DIEGO ARANDOJO

BEATNIK BUENOS AIRES

FACUNDO PERCIO

Fantagraphics  Seattle, Washington

Designer: Justin Allan-Spencer
Editor: Conrad Groth
Production: Paul Baresh
Associate Publisher: Eric Reynolds
Publisher: Gary Groth

This book is typeset in Andralis ND, designed
by publisher Juan Ioannis Andralis.

 Fantagraphics Books, Inc.
7563 Lake City Way NE
Seattle, WA 98115

www.fantagraphics.com
facebook.com/fantagraphics
@fantagraphics.com

ISBN: 978-1-68396-403-2
Library of Congress Control Number: 2020942307
First Fantagraphics Books edition: April 2021
Printed in China

"To my family, and thanks to
Mariano Buscaglia."
— *Diego Arandojo*

"To Nuria and our two sons,
Milo and Polo."
— *Facundo Percio*

CONTENTS

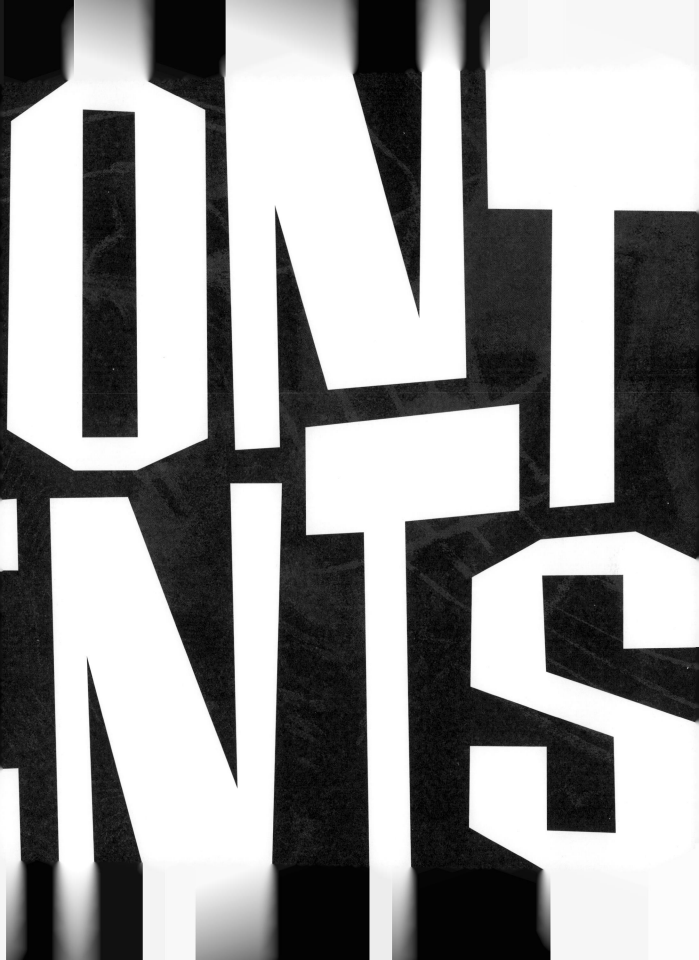

DIEGO ARANDOJO

PRE
FAC

Back in the 1960s, there was another Buenos Aires.

A nocturnal city that competed with its daytime counterpart. A city that sheltered, in its downtown streets and alleyways, an erratic community of artists.

Writers, painters, musicians, sculptors, and performers gathered in cafes, many of them in the area around the Instituto Di Tella (a space for experimentation with and staging of all sorts of conceptual art shows and "crazy acts"). Alone or in groups, they imparted a distinctive vibe to the Buenos Aires night.

This volume is a sort of logbook of that creatively vital period, which has been largely subsumed into the broader cultural history of Argentina. It is a balancing act, at once a faithful reconstruction and an impressionistic, fictionalized account.

When I started making my documentary *Opium: La Argentina beatnik* (*Opium: Beatnik Argentina*), I had the privilege of interviewing the main players in an intense, daring, provocative era. The Opium group defined themselves as "writers who don't write," suggesting that literature isn't always found in books. Since I had so much material and so many anecdotes I was unable to include in the film, I got the idea of collecting them into a graphic novel.

Facundo Percio's somber, evocative art brings that group of vibrant and sometimes mysterious characters to life. Wreathed in cigarette smoke, in a Buenos Aires where anything could happen... and did.

We hope you will enjoy reading this book as much as we enjoyed making it.

chapter ONE: A Fireman

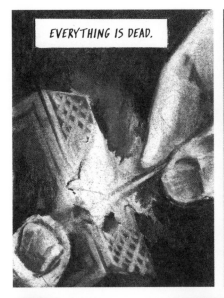

EVERYTHING IS DEAD.

THE SKY. THE EARTH.

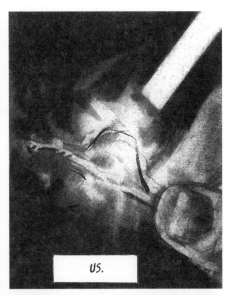

US.

WE ARE WEAK. UNSTABLE.

WE ARE BORN FATED TO DIE.

OUR EXISTENCE IS COLD.

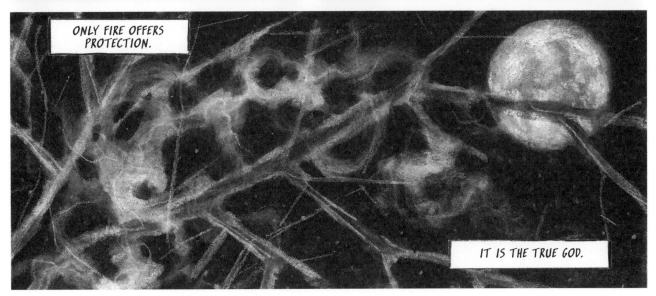

ONLY FIRE OFFERS PROTECTION.

IT IS THE TRUE GOD.

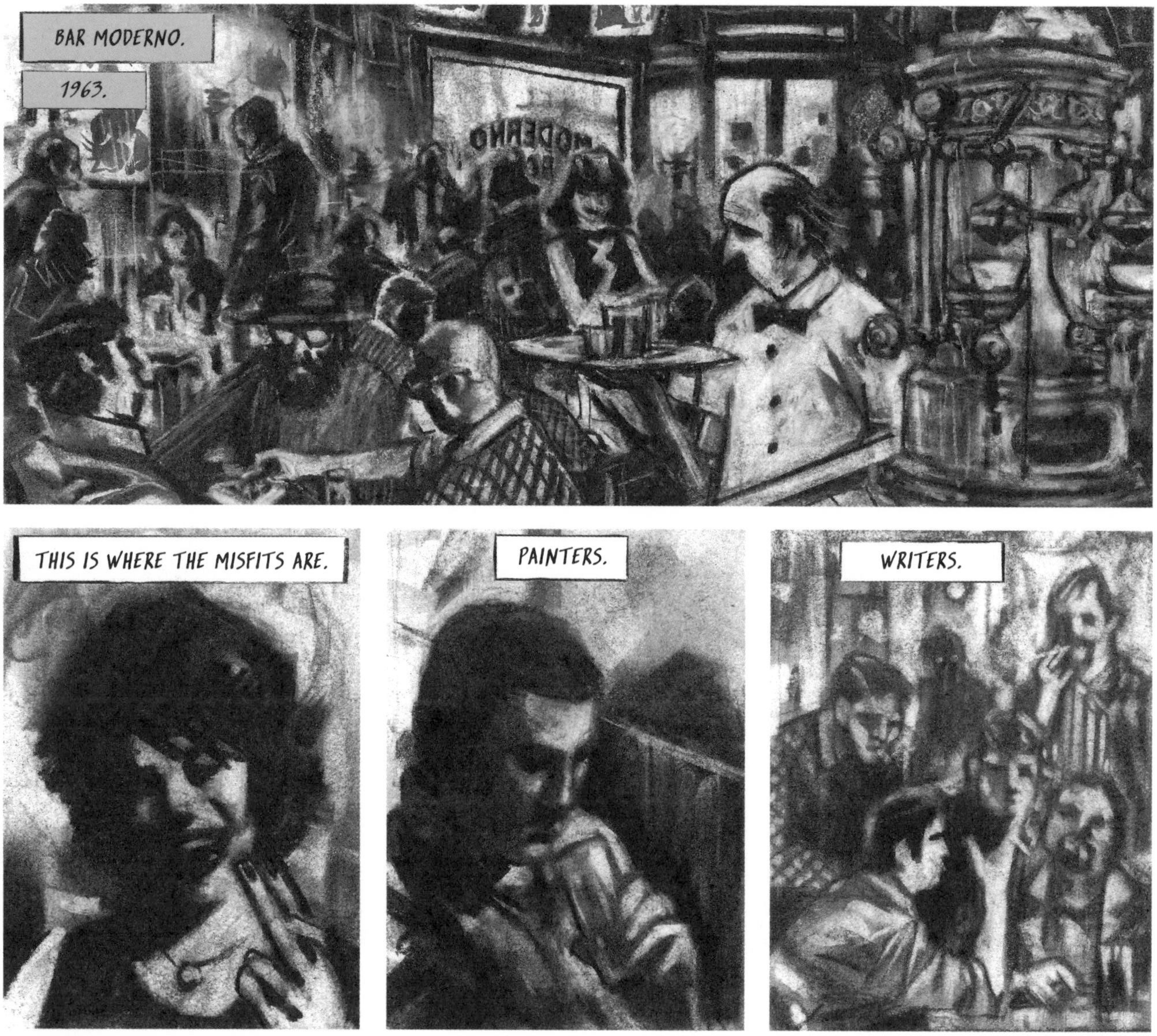
BAR MODERNO.
1963.
THIS IS WHERE THE MISFITS ARE.
PAINTERS.
WRITERS.

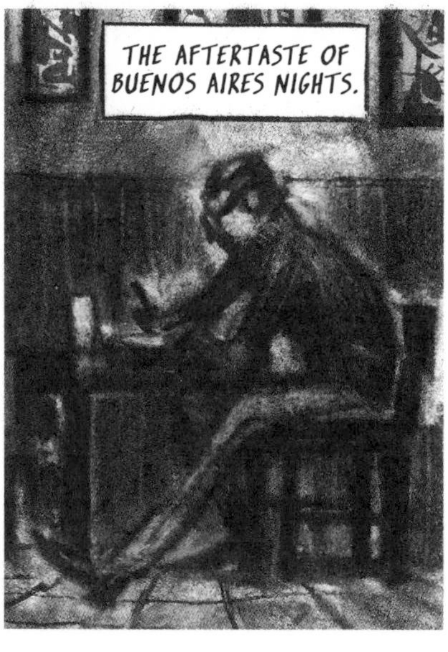
THE AFTERTASTE OF BUENOS AIRES NIGHTS.

Beatnik Buenos Aires

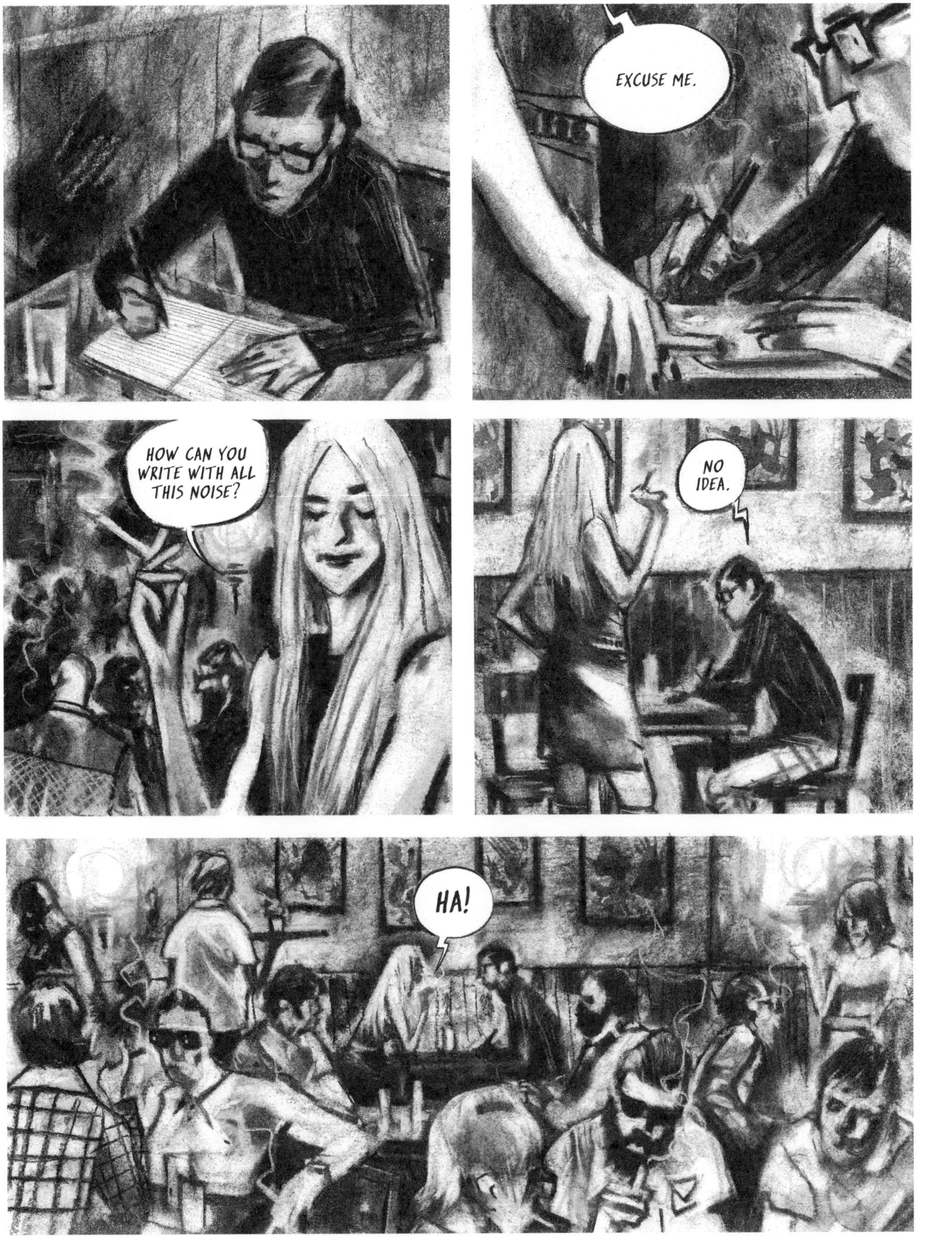
EXCUSE ME.
HOW CAN YOU WRITE WITH ALL THIS NOISE?
NO IDEA.
HA!

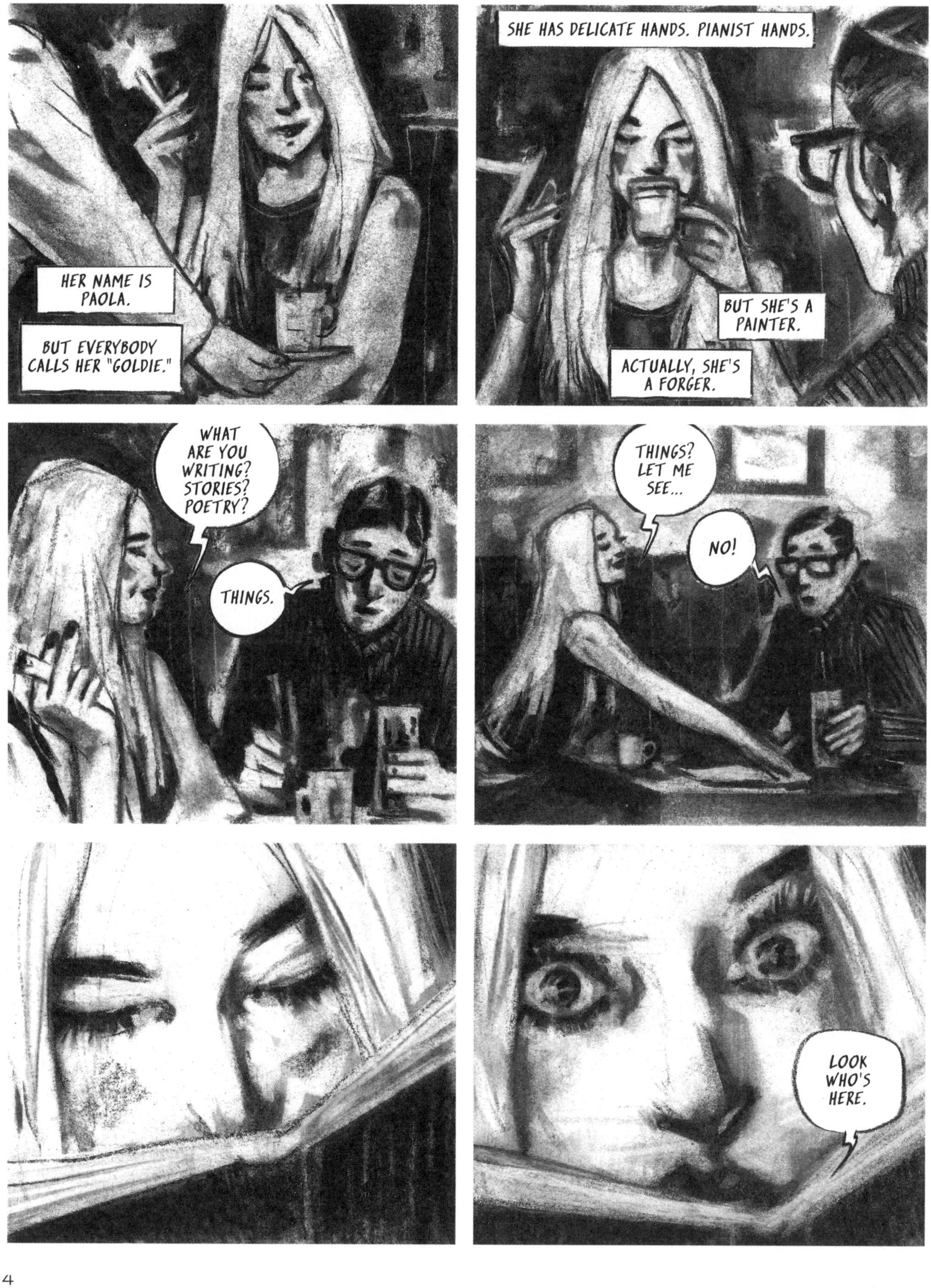
HER NAME IS PAOLA.
BUT EVERYBODY CALLS HER "GOLDIE."
SHE HAS DELICATE HANDS. PIANIST HANDS.
BUT SHE'S A PAINTER.
ACTUALLY, SHE'S A FORGER.
WHAT ARE YOU WRITING? STORIES? POETRY?
THINGS.
THINGS? LET ME SEE...
NO!
LOOK WHO'S HERE.

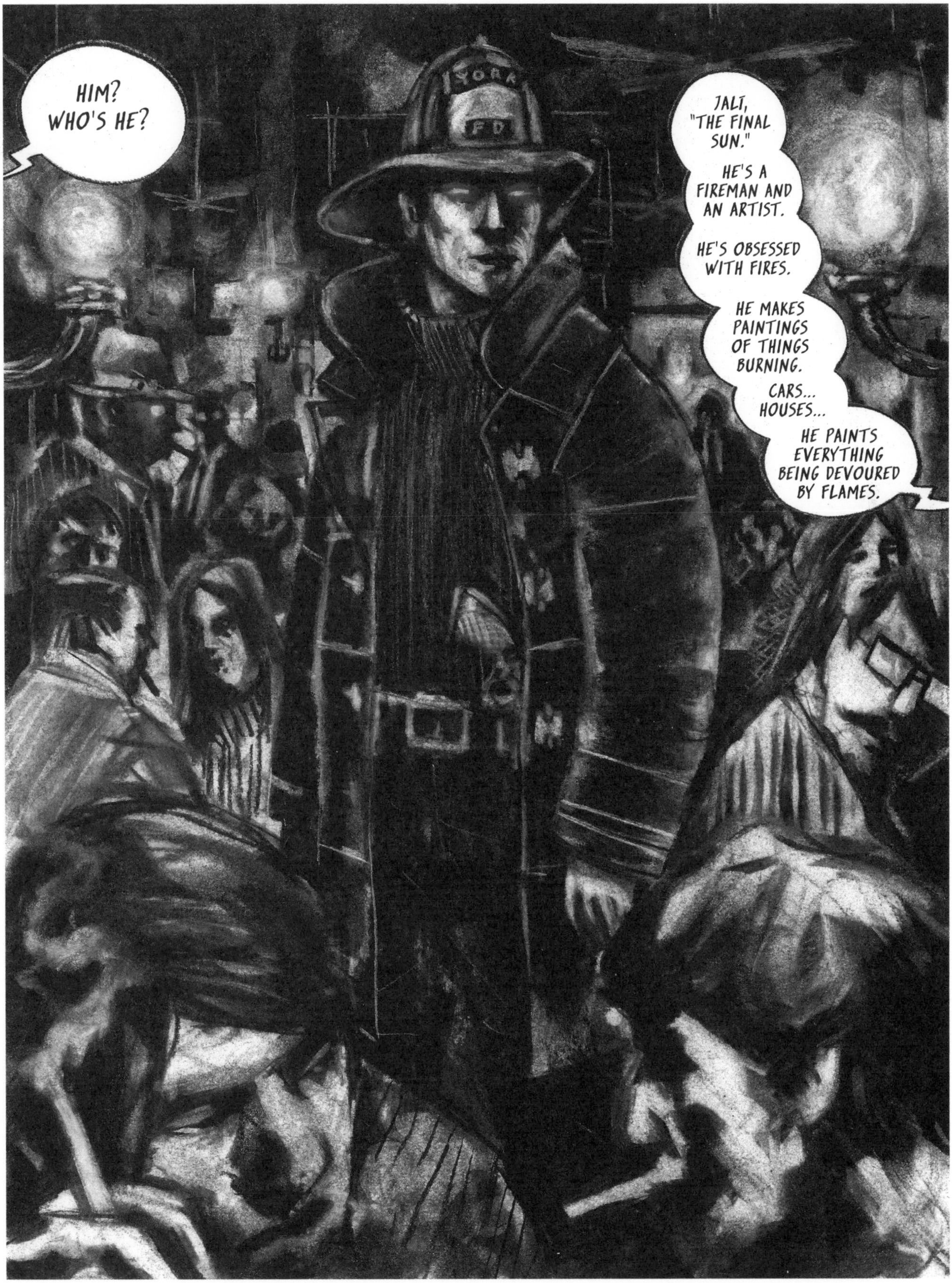
HIM? WHO'S HE?
JALT, "THE FINAL SUN."
HE'S A FIREMAN AND AN ARTIST.
HE'S OBSESSED WITH FIRES.
HE MAKES PAINTINGS OF THINGS BURNING.
CARS... HOUSES...
HE PAINTS EVERYTHING BEING DEVOURED BY FLAMES.
YORK
FD

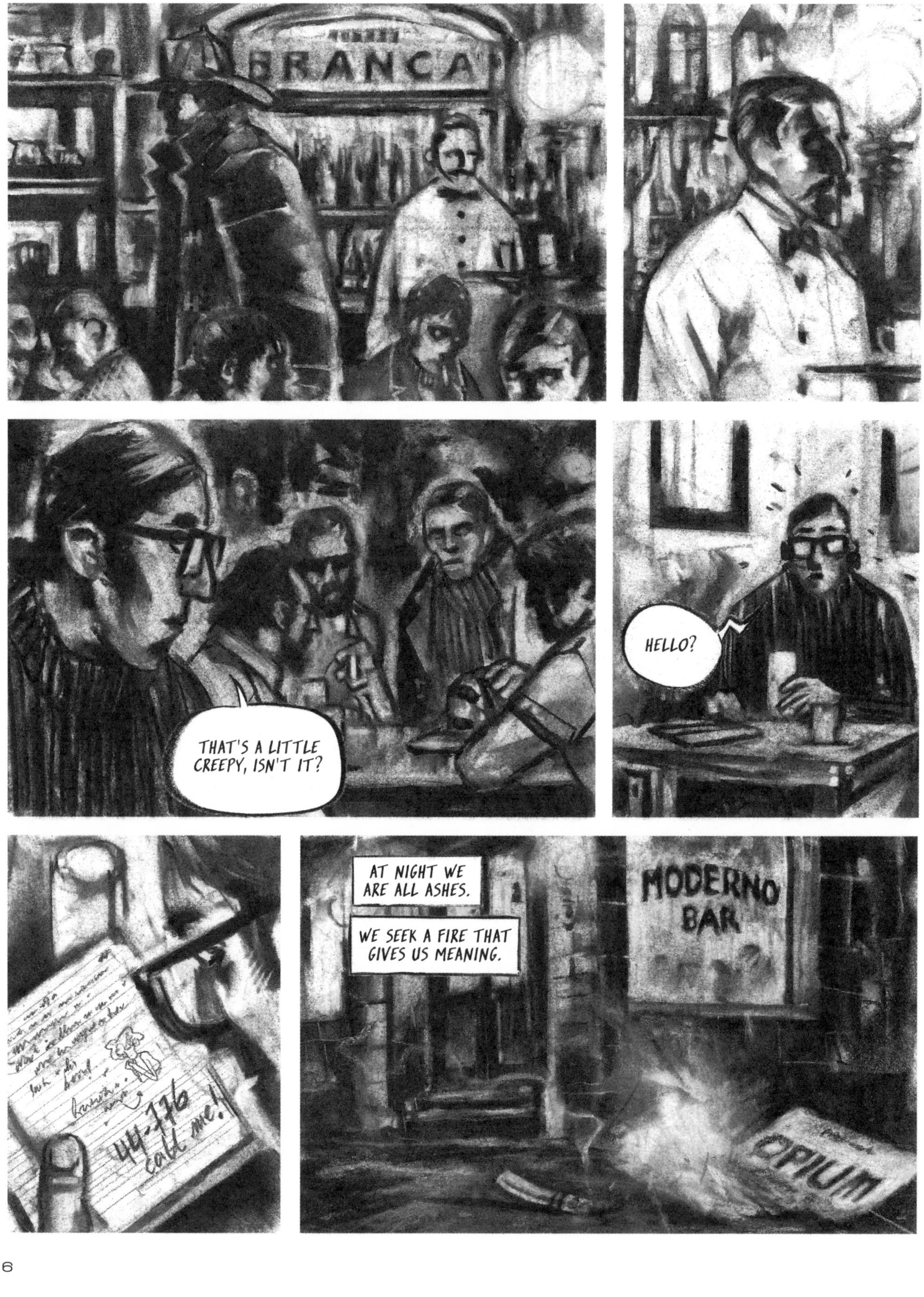
BRANCA
THAT'S A LITTLE CREEPY, ISN'T IT?
HELLO?
44-776 call me!
AT NIGHT WE ARE ALL ASHES.
WE SEEK A FIRE THAT GIVES US MEANING.
MODERNO BAR
OPIUM

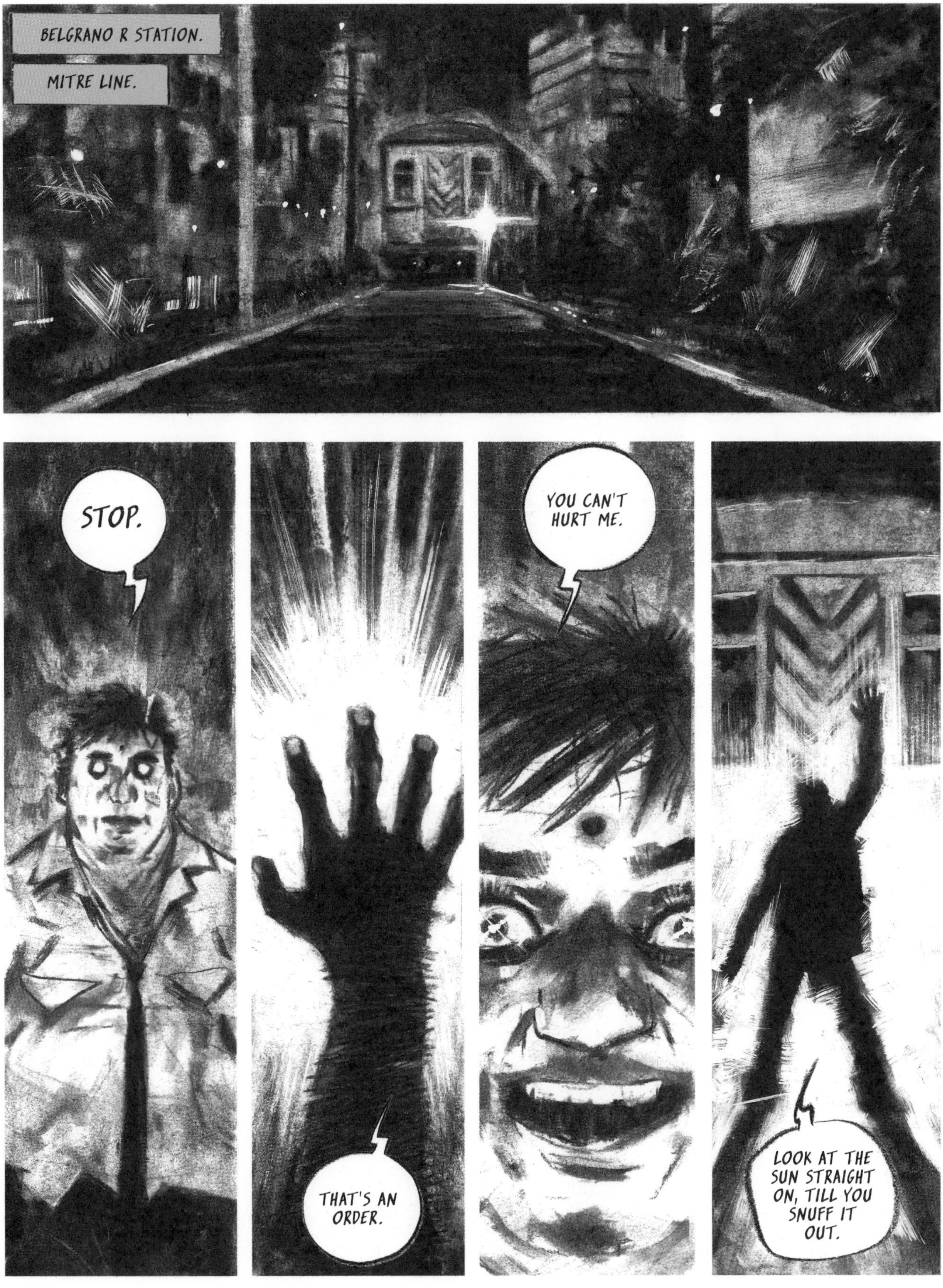
BELGRANO R STATION.
MITRE LINE.
STOP.
THAT'S AN ORDER.
YOU CAN'T HURT ME.
LOOK AT THE SUN STRAIGHT ON, TILL YOU SNUFF IT OUT.

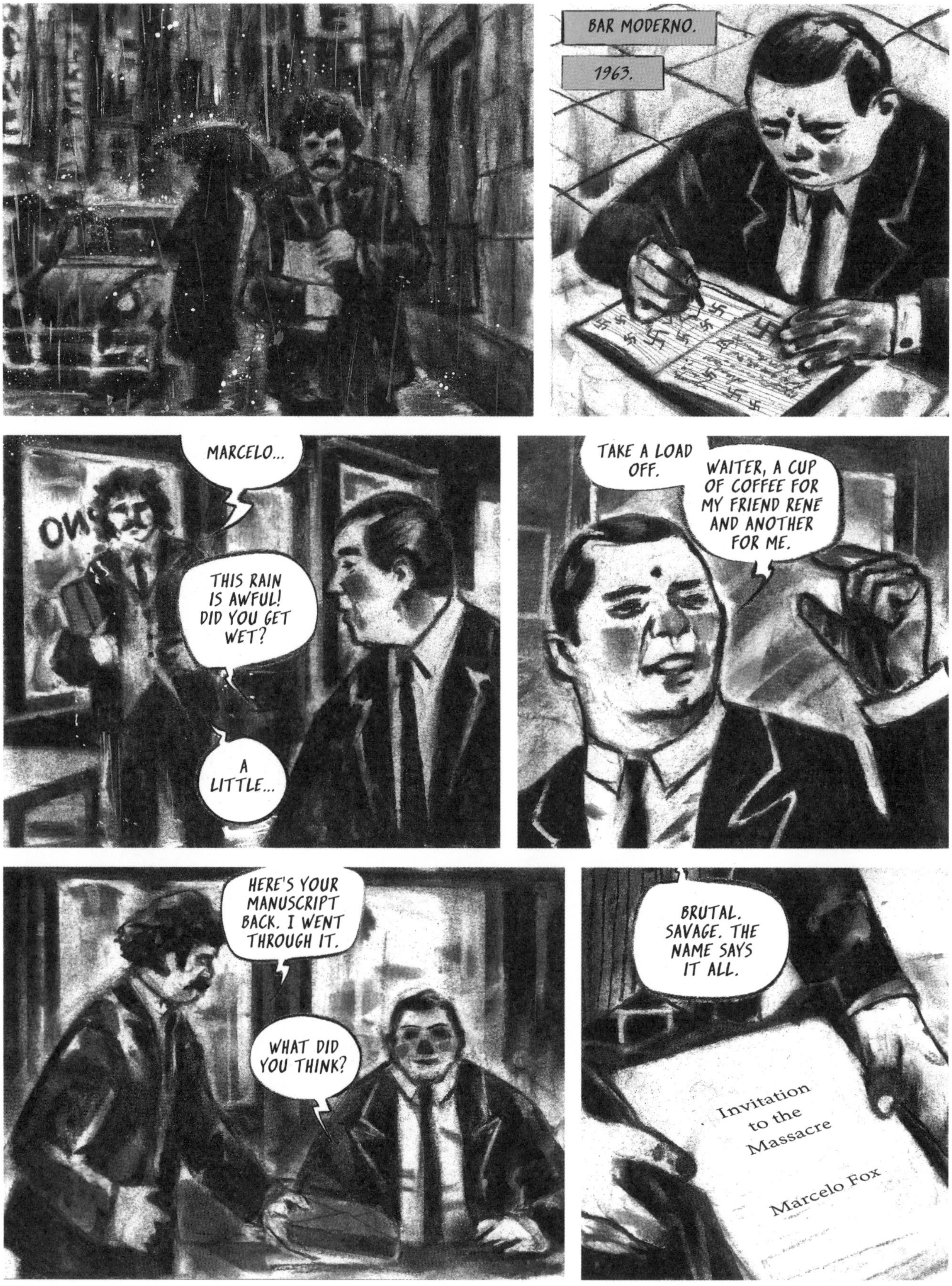
BAR MODERNO.
1963.
MARCELO...
THIS RAIN IS AWFUL! DID YOU GET WET?
A LITTLE...
TAKE A LOAD OFF.
WAITER, A CUP OF COFFEE FOR MY FRIEND RENE AND ANOTHER FOR ME.
HERE'S YOUR MANUSCRIPT BACK. I WENT THROUGH IT.
WHAT DID YOU THINK?
BRUTAL. SAVAGE. THE NAME SAYS IT ALL.
Invitation to the Massacre
Marcelo Fox

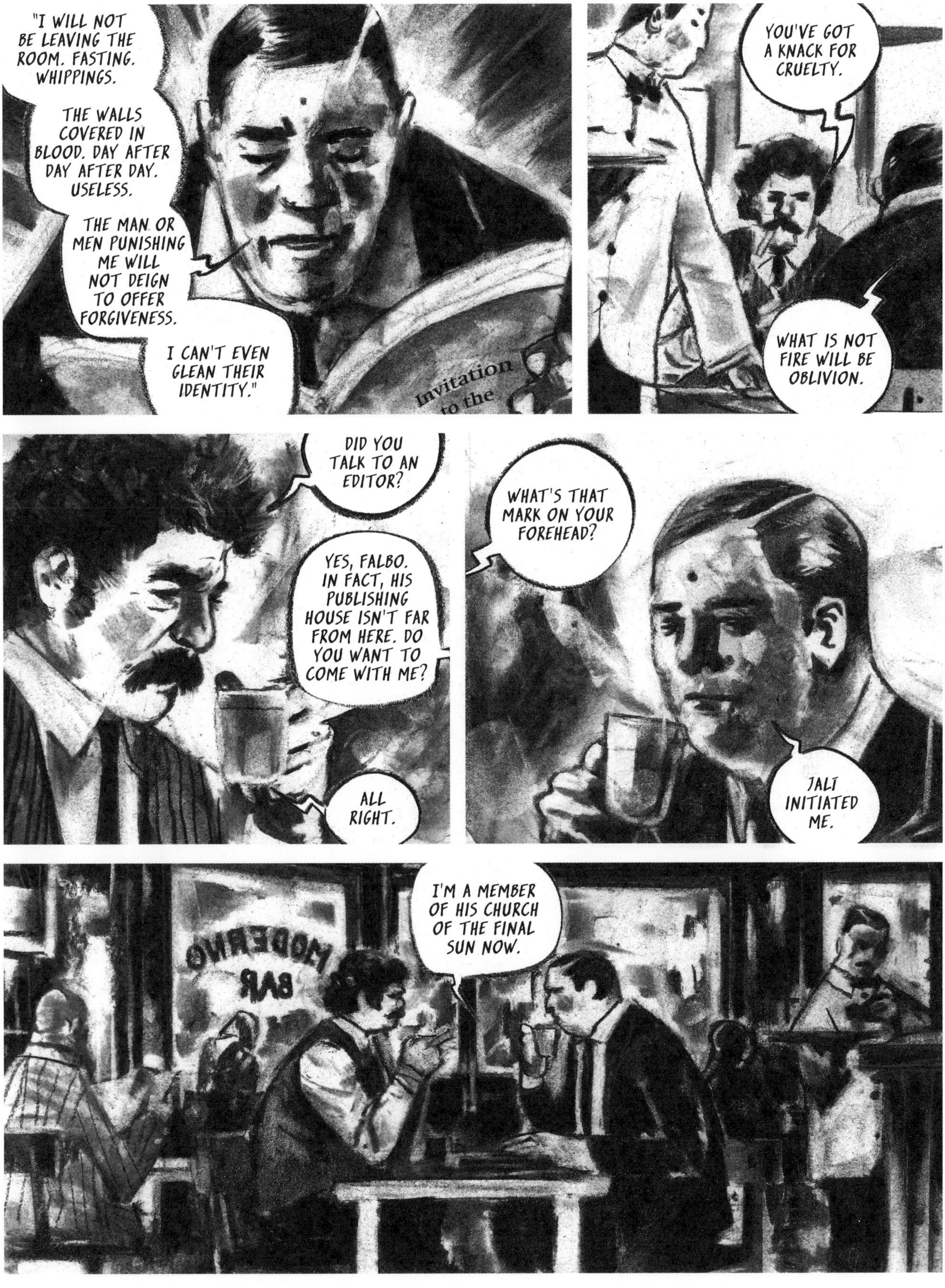
"I WILL NOT BE LEAVING THE ROOM. FASTING. WHIPPINGS.
THE WALLS COVERED IN BLOOD. DAY AFTER DAY AFTER DAY. USELESS.
THE MAN OR MEN PUNISHING ME WILL NOT DEIGN TO OFFER FORGIVENESS.
I CAN'T EVEN GLEAN THEIR IDENTITY."
Invitation to the
YOU'VE GOT A KNACK FOR CRUELTY.
WHAT IS NOT FIRE WILL BE OBLIVION.
DID YOU TALK TO AN EDITOR?
YES, FALBO. IN FACT, HIS PUBLISHING HOUSE ISN'T FAR FROM HERE. DO YOU WANT TO COME WITH ME?
ALL RIGHT.
WHAT'S THAT MARK ON YOUR FOREHEAD?
JALT INITIATED ME.
I'M A MEMBER OF HIS CHURCH OF THE FINAL SUN NOW.
MODERNO BAR

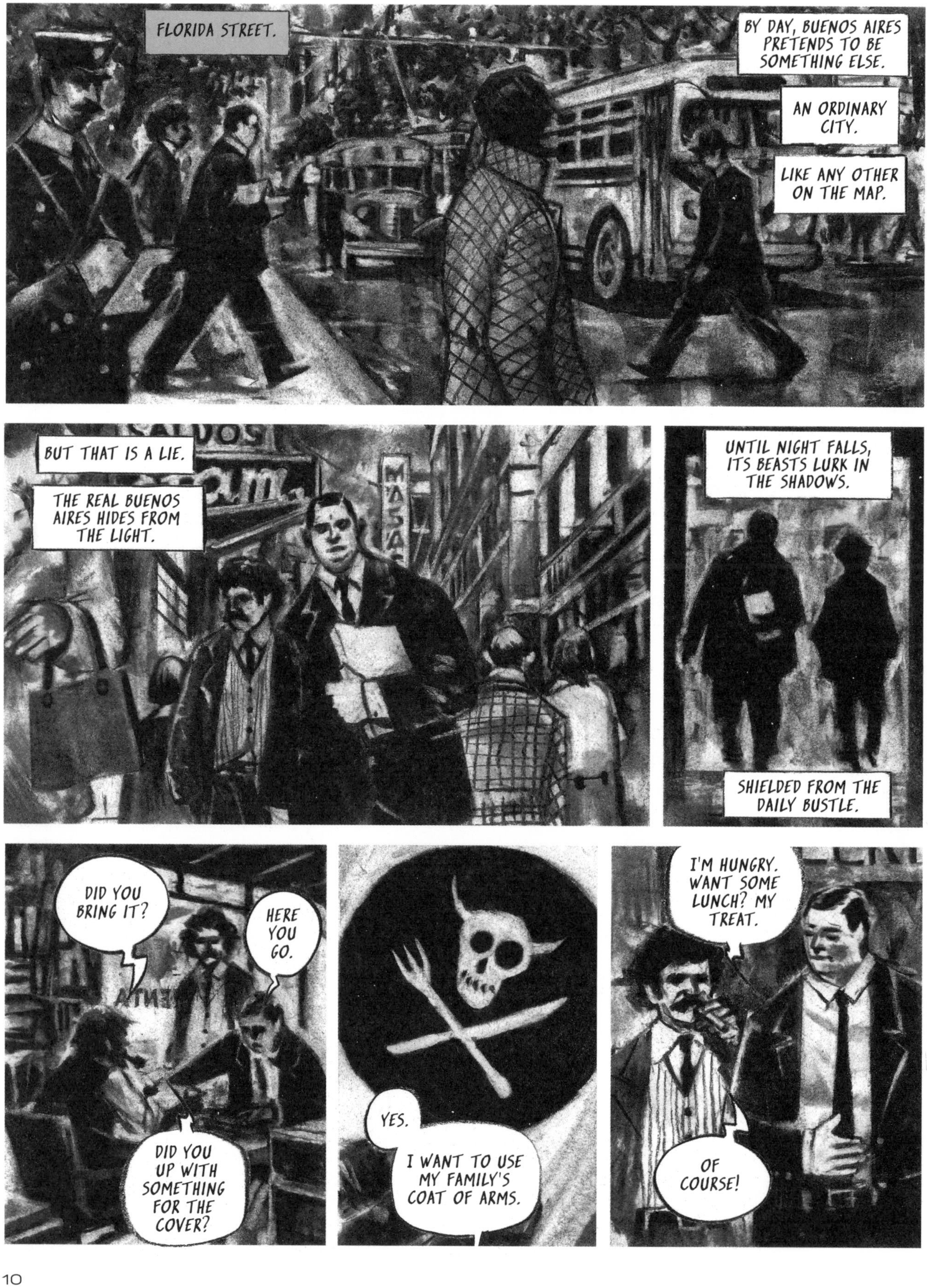
FLORIDA STREET.
BY DAY, BUENOS AIRES PRETENDS TO BE SOMETHING ELSE.
AN ORDINARY CITY.
LIKE ANY OTHER ON THE MAP.
BUT THAT IS A LIE.
THE REAL BUENOS AIRES HIDES FROM THE LIGHT.
UNTIL NIGHT FALLS, ITS BEASTS LURK IN THE SHADOWS.
SHIELDED FROM THE DAILY BUSTLE.
DID YOU BRING IT?
HERE YOU GO.
DID YOU UP WITH SOMETHING FOR THE COVER?
YES.
I WANT TO USE MY FAMILY'S COAT OF ARMS.
I'M HUNGRY. WANT SOME LUNCH? MY TREAT.
OF COURSE!

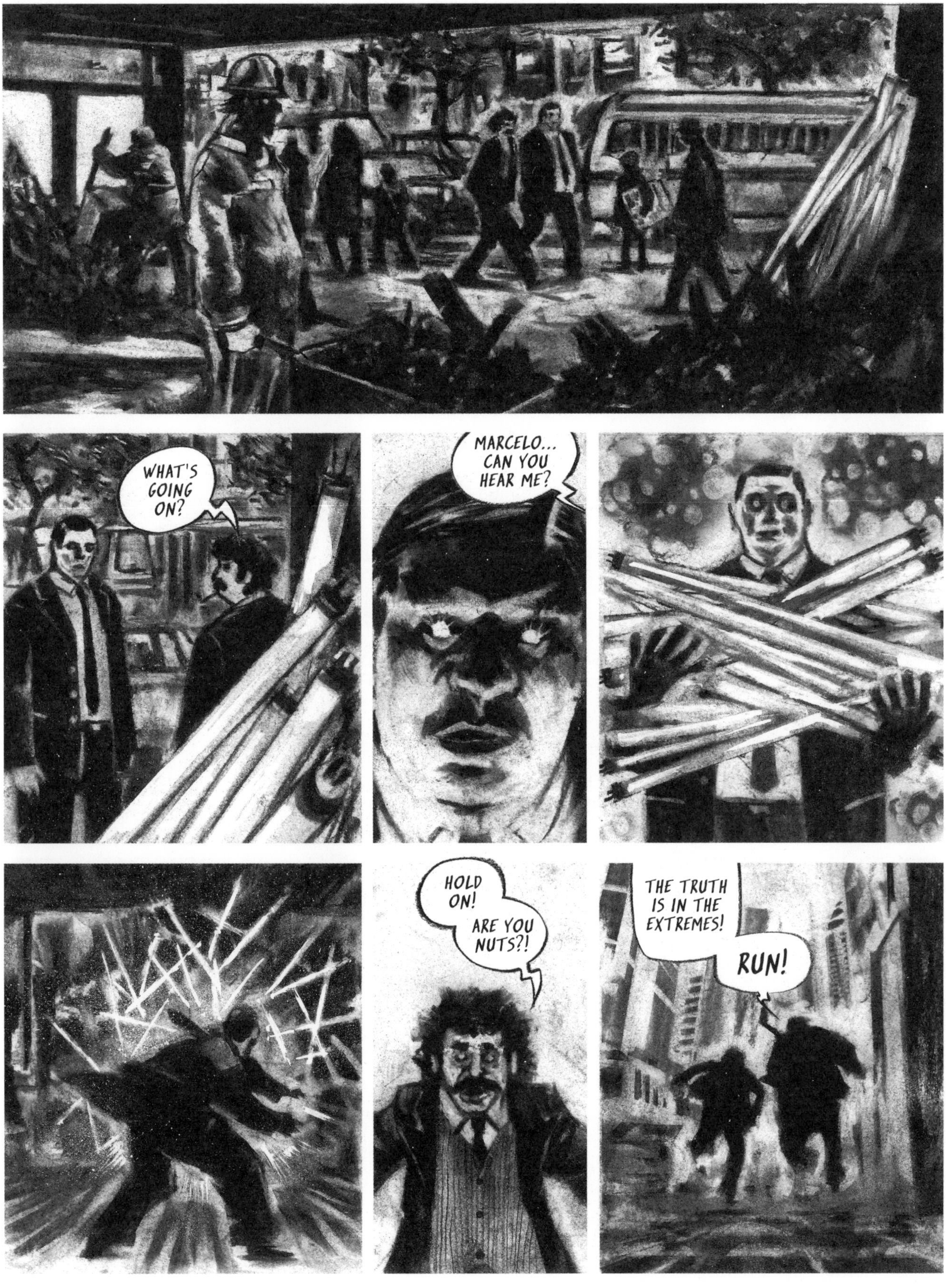
WHAT'S GOING ON?
MARCELO... CAN YOU HEAR ME?
HOLD ON!
ARE YOU NUTS?!
THE TRUTH IS IN THE EXTREMES!
RUN!

HA HA HA!

YOU HAVE TO LOOK AT THE SUN STRAIGHT ON, TILL YOU SNUFF IT OUT.

STEADILY. WITHOUT FEAR.

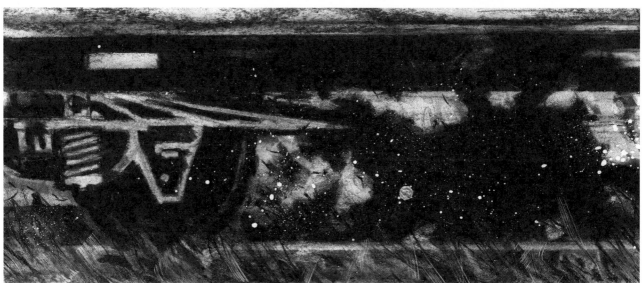

AAAAAH!

BECAUSE THE TIME GIVEN TO HUMANKIND IS SHORT.

THOUGH THERE WILL ALWAYS BE THOSE WHO DREAM OF POSSESSING THE ABSOLUTE.

chapter THREE: The Angel of Death

YOU HAVE TO KNOW HOW TO WAIT.

THE PRECISE MOMENT.

AND WHEN IT COMES, YOU HAVE TO ACT FAST.

BECAUSE LIGHT IS A TRICKY THING.

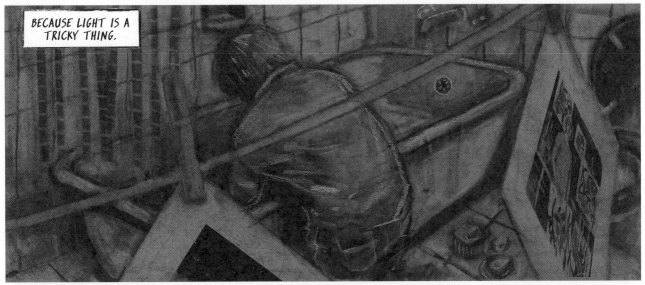

IT MAKES THE IMAGE WE SEEK...

...BUT IT CAN ALSO ERASE IT FOR GOOD.

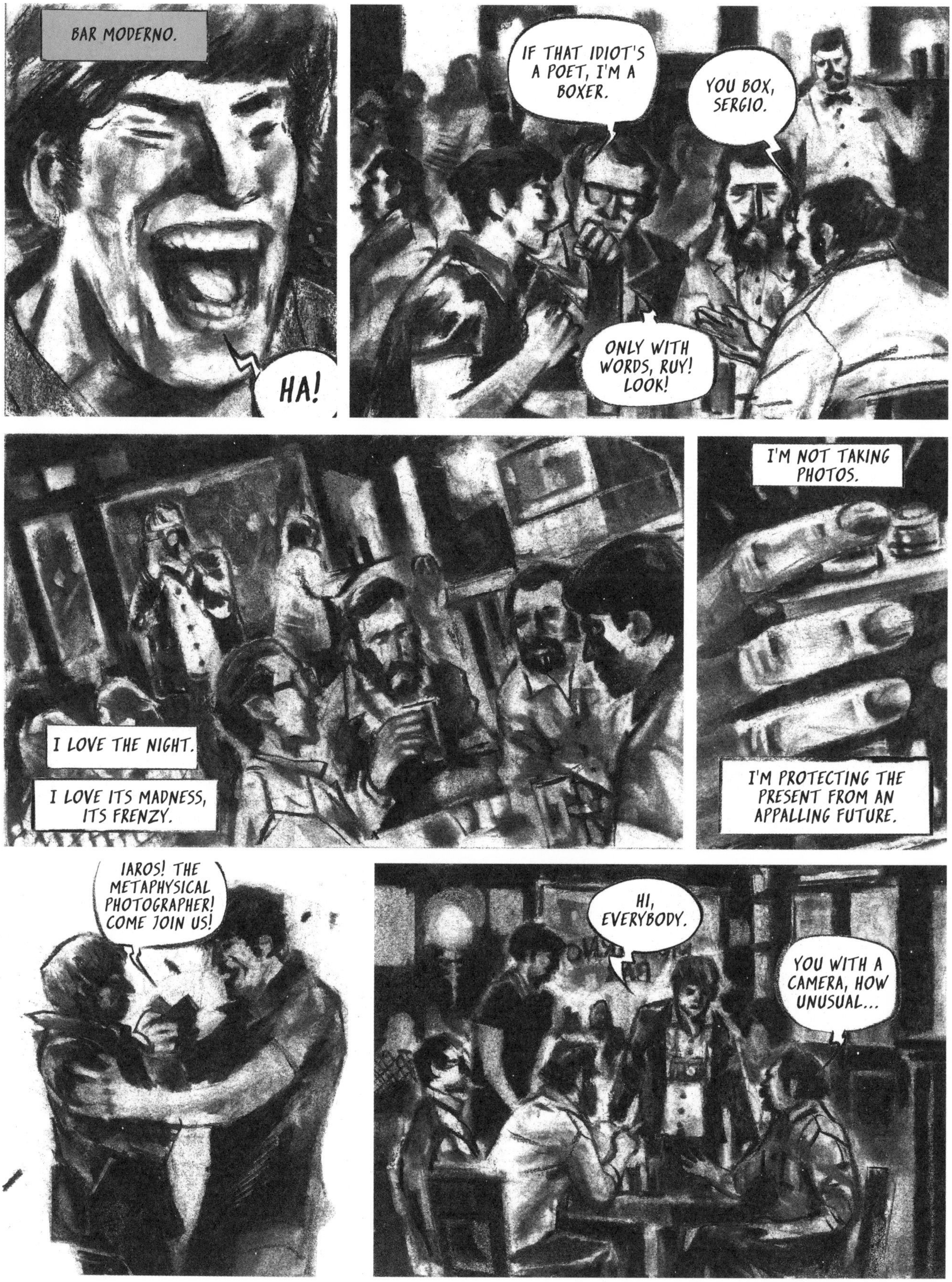
BAR MODERNO.
HA!
IF THAT IDIOT'S A POET, I'M A BOXER.
YOU BOX, SERGIO.
ONLY WITH WORDS, RUY! LOOK!
I LOVE THE NIGHT.
I LOVE ITS MADNESS, ITS FRENZY.
I'M NOT TAKING PHOTOS.
I'M PROTECTING THE PRESENT FROM AN APPALLING FUTURE.
IAROS! THE METAPHYSICAL PHOTOGRAPHER! COME JOIN US!
HI, EVERYBODY.
YOU WITH A CAMERA, HOW UNUSUAL...

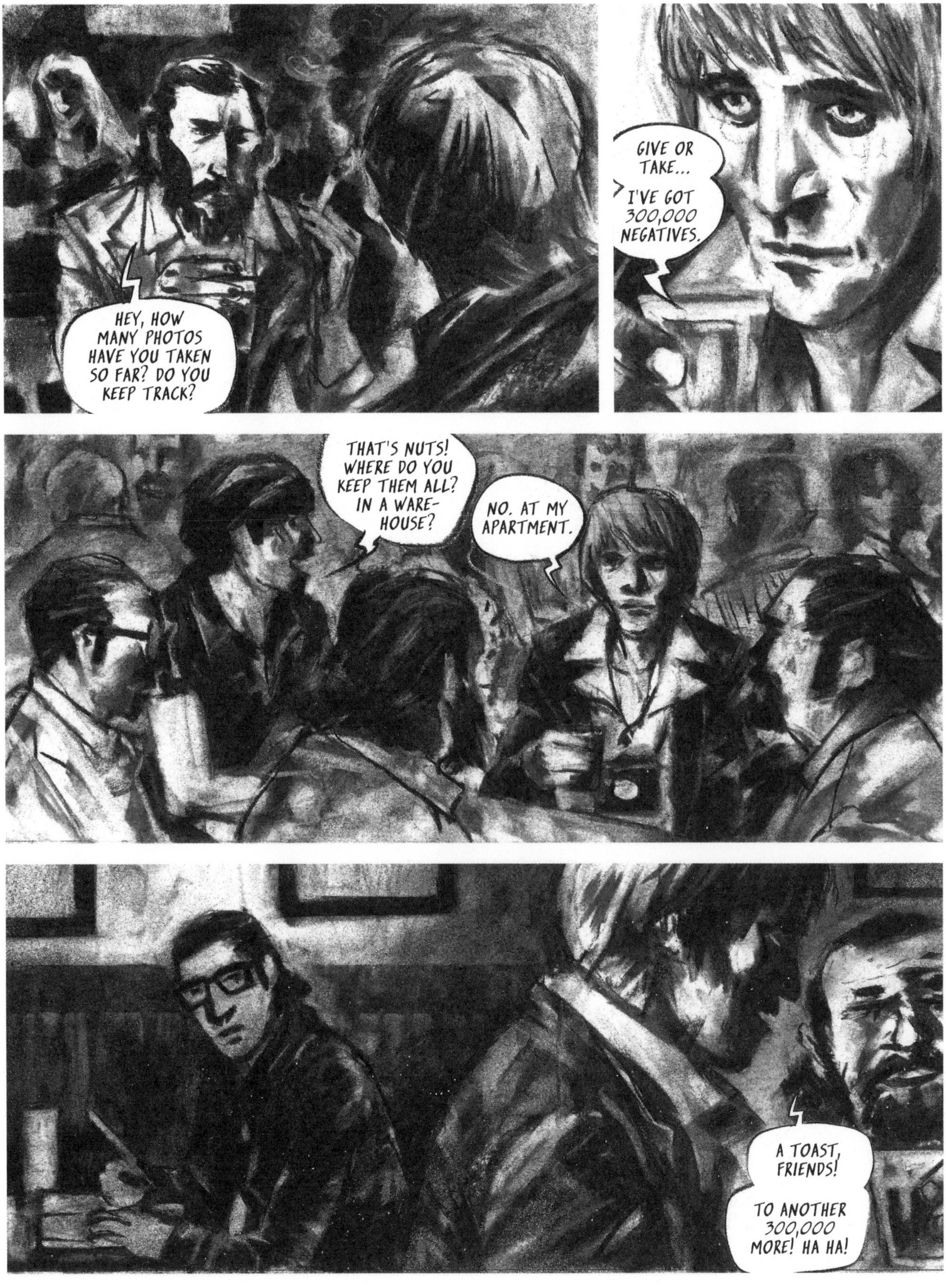
HEY, HOW MANY PHOTOS HAVE YOU TAKEN SO FAR? DO YOU KEEP TRACK?
GIVE OR TAKE...
I'VE GOT 300,000 NEGATIVES.
THAT'S NUTS! WHERE DO YOU KEEP THEM ALL? IN A WARE-HOUSE?
NO. AT MY APARTMENT.
A TOAST, FRIENDS!
TO ANOTHER 300,000 MORE! HA HA!

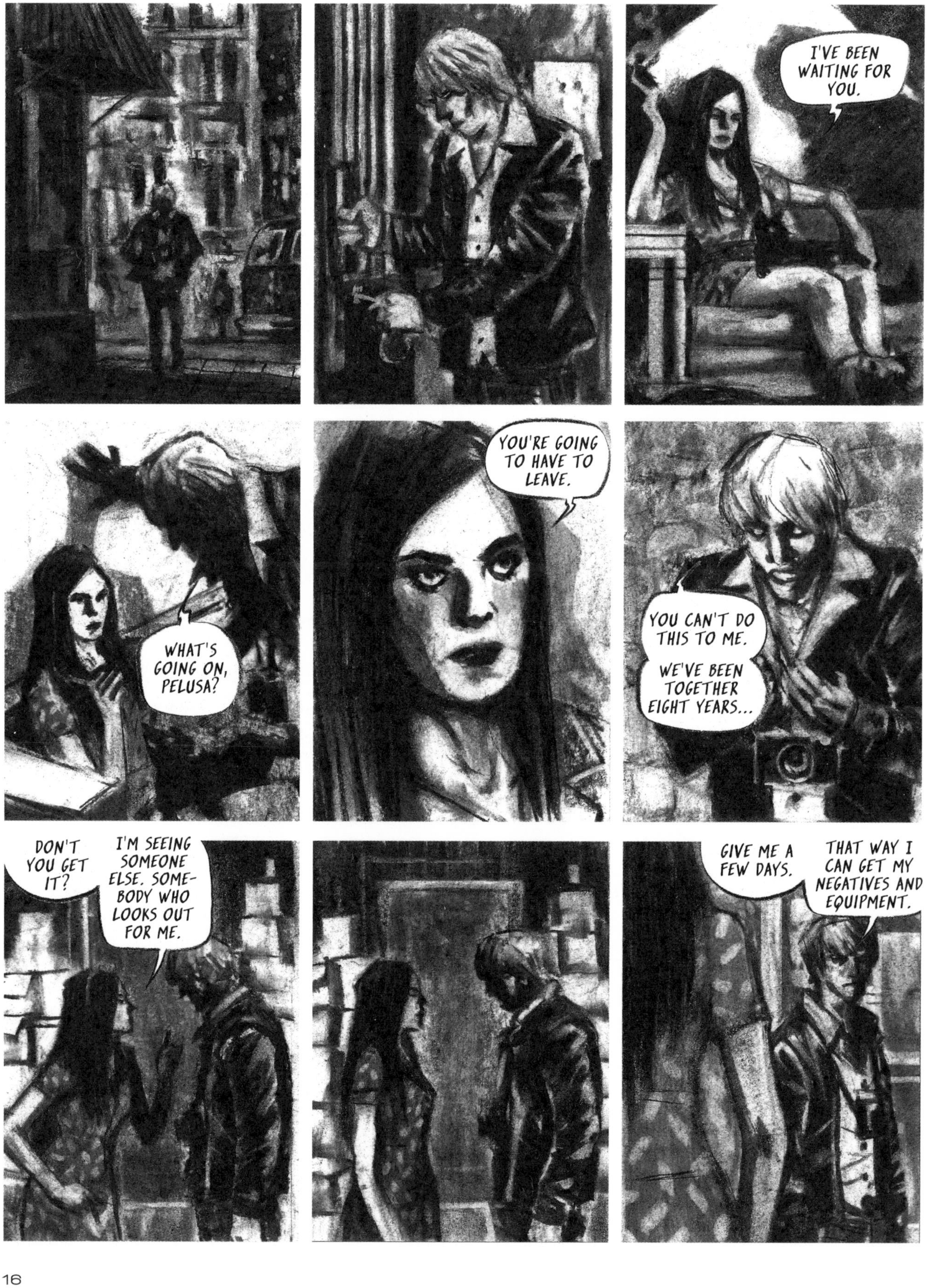
I'VE BEEN WAITING FOR YOU.
WHAT'S GOING ON, PELUSA?
YOU'RE GOING TO HAVE TO LEAVE.
YOU CAN'T DO THIS TO ME.
WE'VE BEEN TOGETHER EIGHT YEARS...
DON'T YOU GET IT?
I'M SEEING SOMEONE ELSE. SOMEBODY WHO LOOKS OUT FOR ME.
GIVE ME A FEW DAYS.
THAT WAY I CAN GET MY NEGATIVES AND EQUIPMENT.

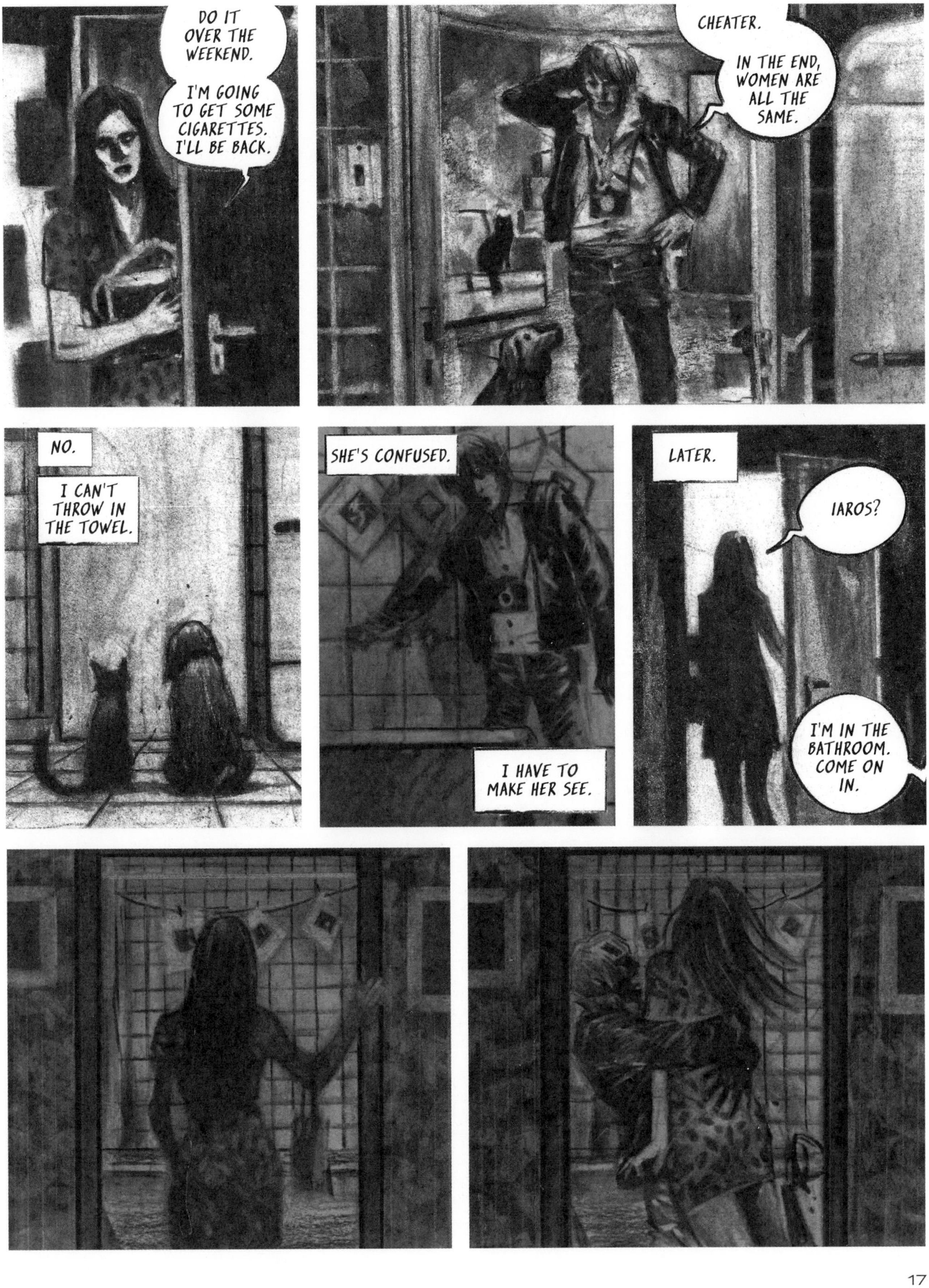
DO IT OVER THE WEEKEND.
I'M GOING TO GET SOME CIGARETTES. I'LL BE BACK.
CHEATER.
IN THE END, WOMEN ARE ALL THE SAME.
NO.
I CAN'T THROW IN THE TOWEL.
SHE'S CONFUSED.
I HAVE TO MAKE HER SEE.
LATER.
IAROS?
I'M IN THE BATHROOM. COME ON IN.

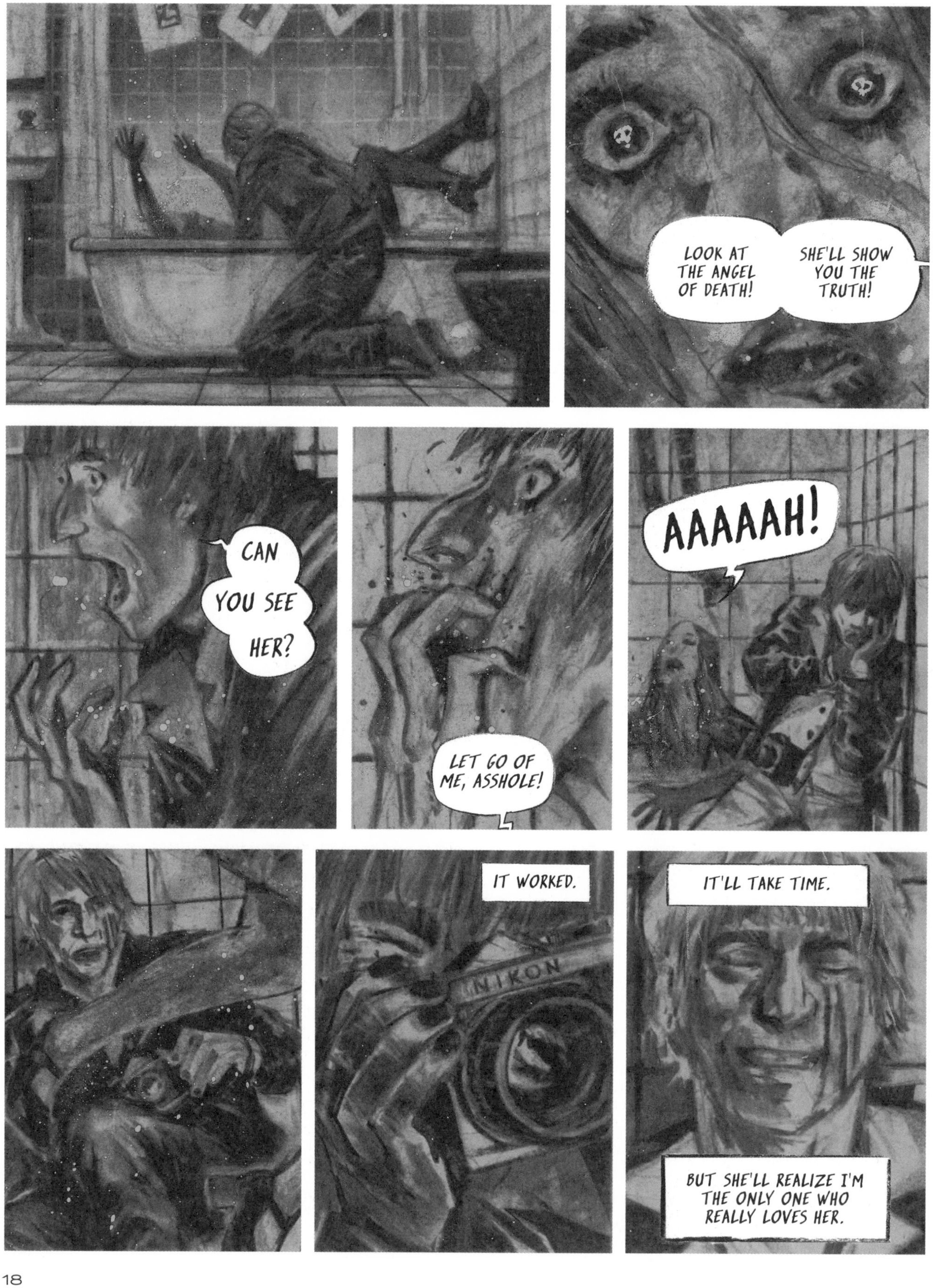
LOOK AT THE ANGEL OF DEATH!
SHE'LL SHOW YOU THE TRUTH!
CAN
YOU SEE
HER?
LET GO OF ME, ASSHOLE!
AAAAAH!
IT WORKED.
NIKON
IT'LL TAKE TIME.
BUT SHE'LL REALIZE I'M THE ONLY ONE WHO REALLY LOVES HER.

chapter FOUR: Exact Copy

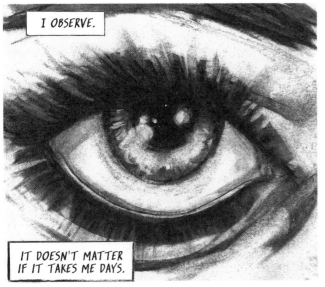

I OBSERVE.

IT DOESN'T MATTER IF IT TAKES ME DAYS.

I OBSERVE.

I STUDY THE WORK.

EVERY INCH OF IT.

I TRANSFER IT, BIT BY BIT, INTO MY BRAIN.

I REMEMBER THE COLORS. THE LINES. THE STYLE.

BY THE END OF THE EXERCISE, I'M WIPED OUT.

I REST.

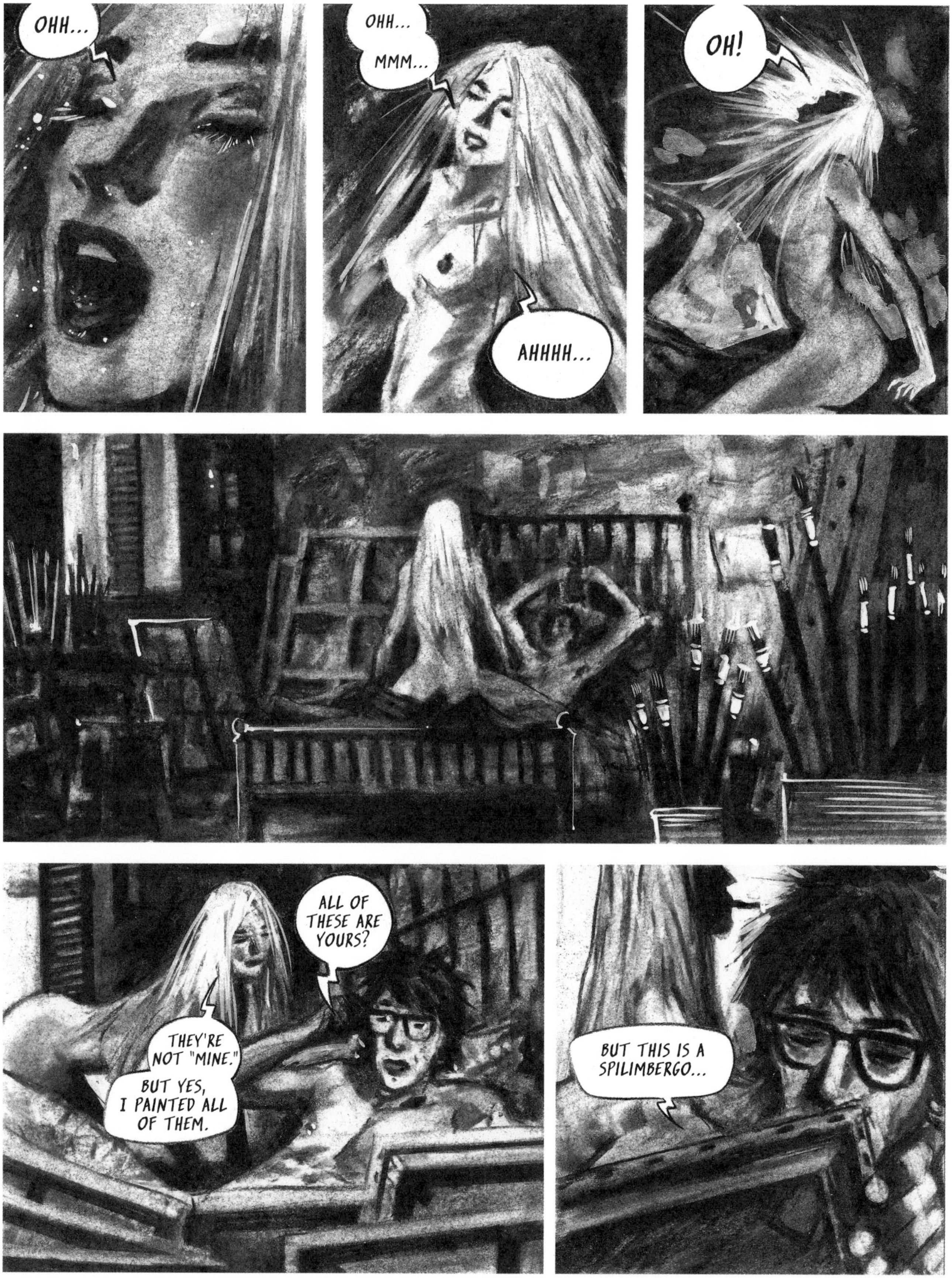
OHH...
OHH...
MMM...
AHHHH...
OH!
ALL OF THESE ARE YOURS?
THEY'RE NOT "MINE."
BUT YES, I PAINTED ALL OF THEM.
BUT THIS IS A SPILIMBERGO...

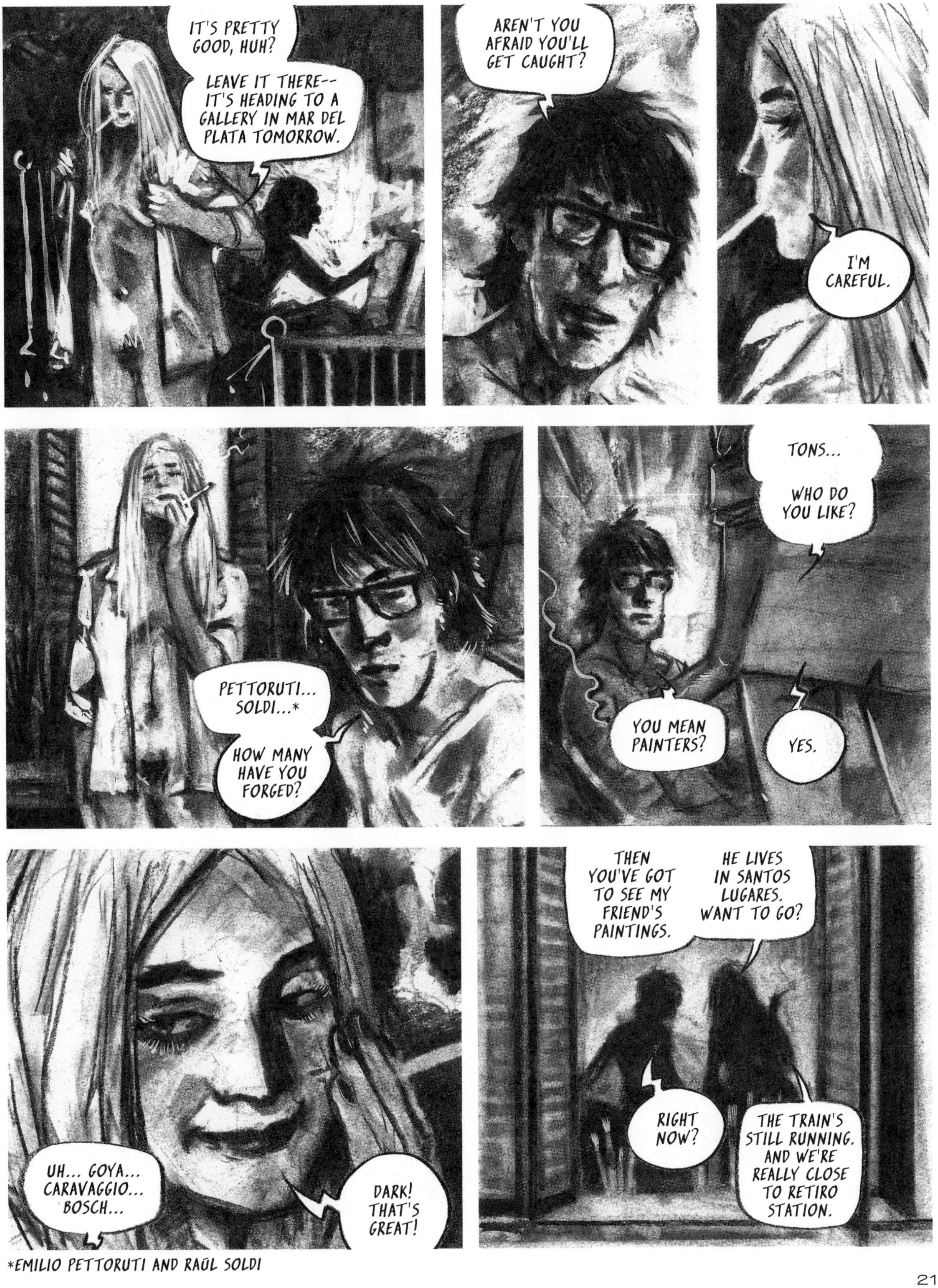
IT'S PRETTY GOOD, HUH?
LEAVE IT THERE-- IT'S HEADING TO A GALLERY IN MAR DEL PLATA TOMORROW.
AREN'T YOU AFRAID YOU'LL GET CAUGHT?
I'M CAREFUL.
PETTORUTI... SOLDI...*
HOW MANY HAVE YOU FORGED?
TONS...
WHO DO YOU LIKE?
YOU MEAN PAINTERS?
YES.
UH... GOYA... CARAVAGGIO... BOSCH...
DARK! THAT'S GREAT!
THEN YOU'VE GOT TO SEE MY FRIEND'S PAINTINGS.
HE LIVES IN SANTOS LUGARES. WANT TO GO?
RIGHT NOW?
THE TRAIN'S STILL RUNNING. AND WE'RE REALLY CLOSE TO RETIRO STATION.

*EMILIO PETTORUTI AND RAÚL SOLDI

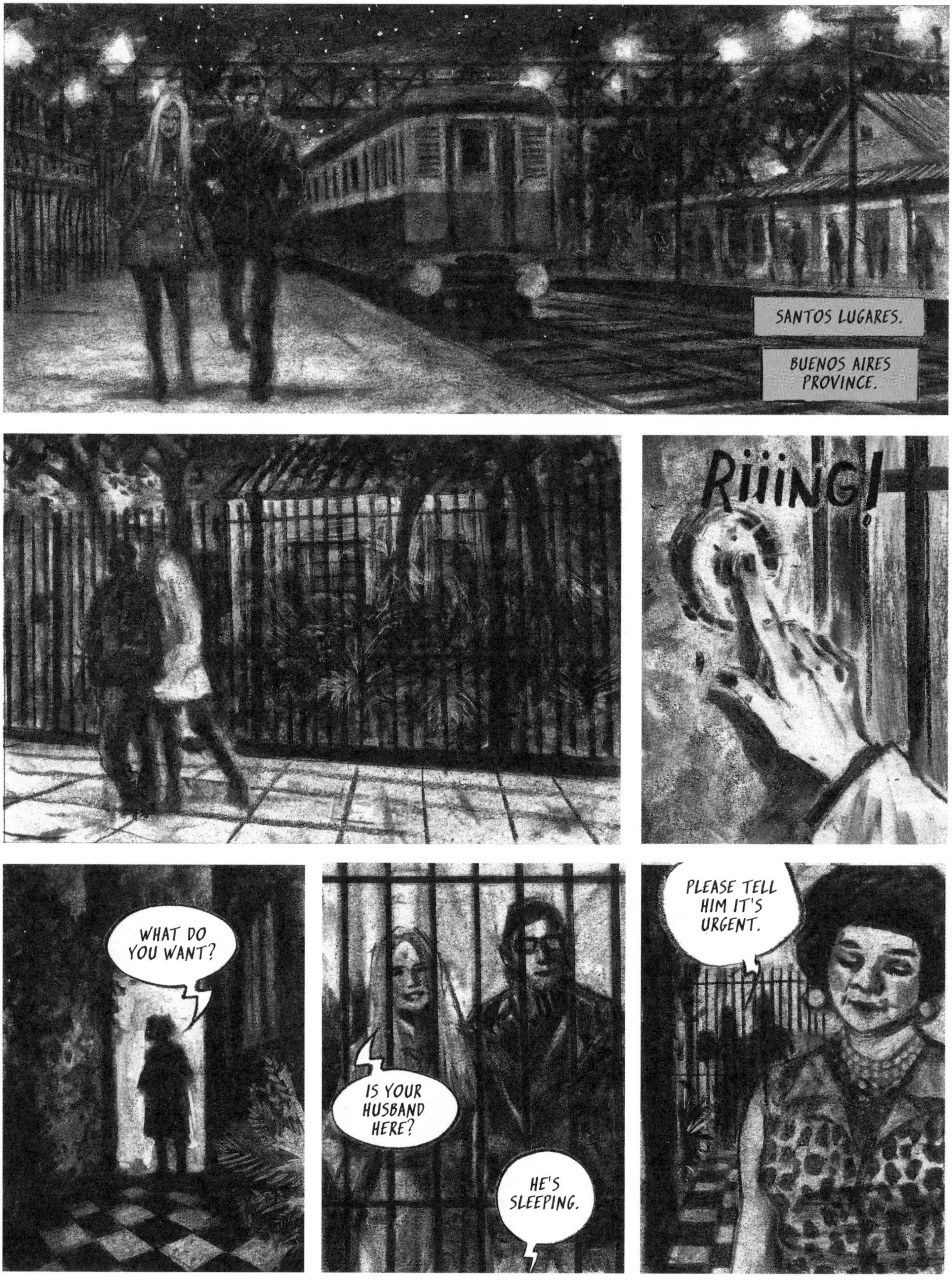
SANTOS LUGARES.
BUENOS AIRES PROVINCE.
RIIING!
WHAT DO YOU WANT?
IS YOUR HUSBAND HERE?
HE'S SLEEPING.
PLEASE TELL HIM IT'S URGENT.

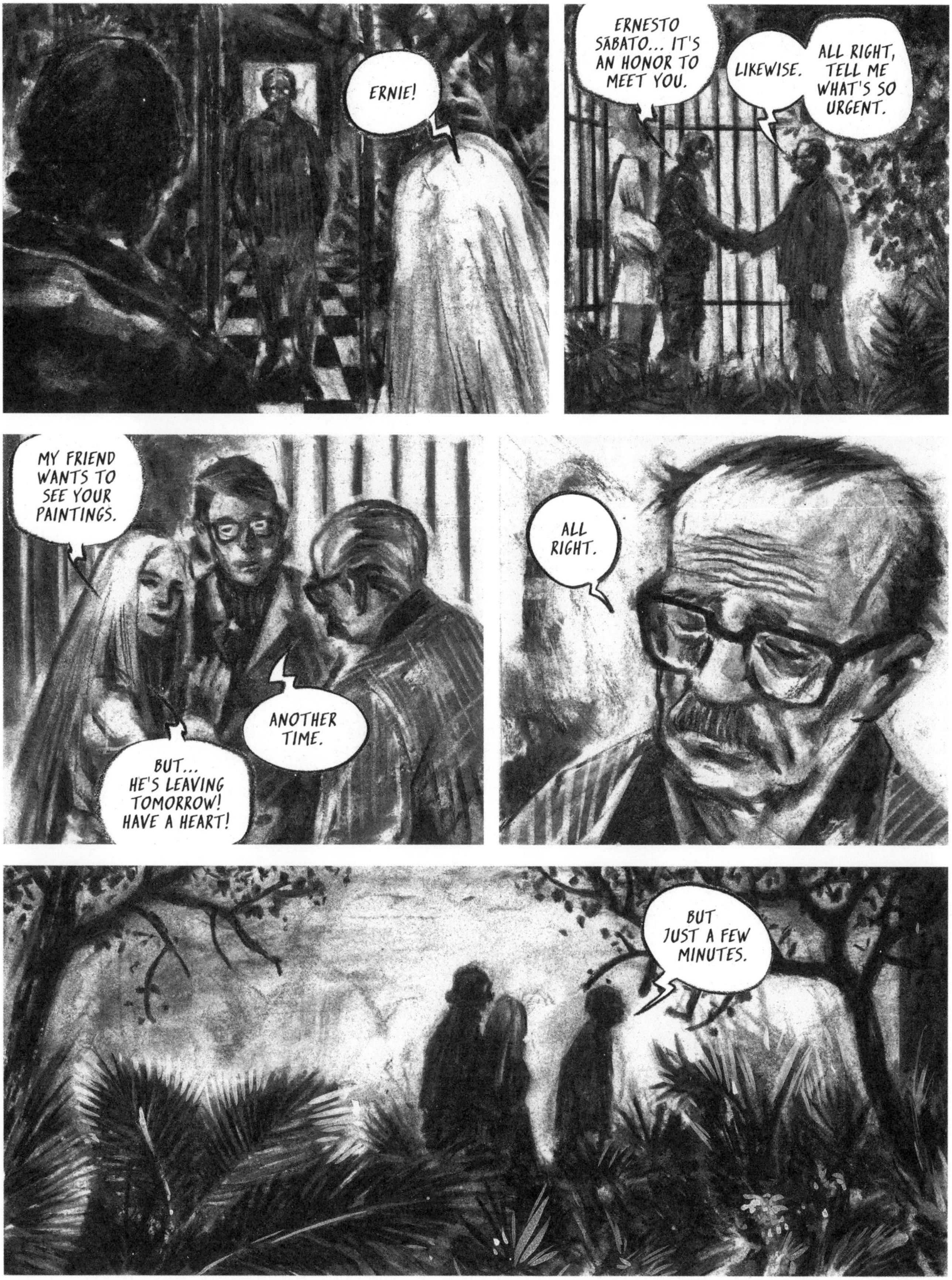
ERNIE!
ERNESTO SÁBATO... IT'S AN HONOR TO MEET YOU.
LIKEWISE.
ALL RIGHT, TELL ME WHAT'S SO URGENT.
MY FRIEND WANTS TO SEE YOUR PAINTINGS.
ANOTHER TIME.
BUT... HE'S LEAVING TOMORROW! HAVE A HEART!
ALL RIGHT.
BUT JUST A FEW MINUTES.

PAINTING IS EXORCISM.

IT ALLOWS US TO EXPEL DEMONS.

TRAP THEM ON THE CANVAS.

TO ADMIRE THEM LATER.

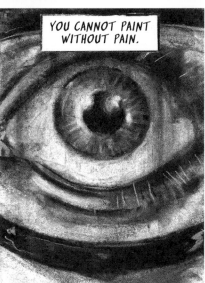

YOU CANNOT PAINT WITHOUT PAIN.

chapter FIVE: Howl

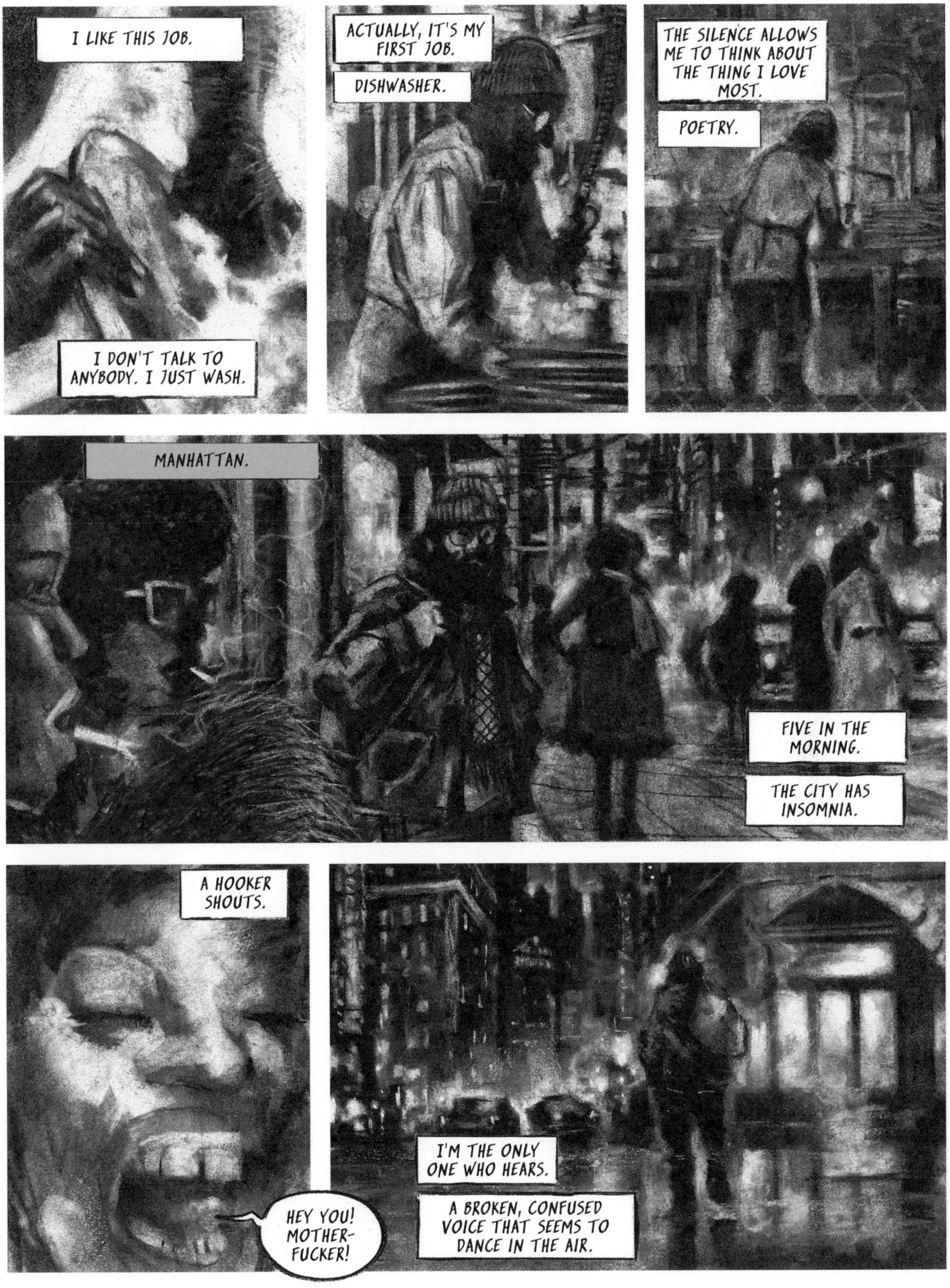

I LIKE THIS JOB.
I DON'T TALK TO ANYBODY. I JUST WASH.
ACTUALLY, IT'S MY FIRST JOB.
DISHWASHER.
THE SILENCE ALLOWS ME TO THINK ABOUT THE THING I LOVE MOST.
POETRY.
MANHATTAN.
FIVE IN THE MORNING.
THE CITY HAS INSOMNIA.
A HOOKER SHOUTS.
HEY YOU! MOTHER-FUCKER!
I'M THE ONLY ONE WHO HEARS.
A BROKEN, CONFUSED VOICE THAT SEEMS TO DANCE IN THE AIR.

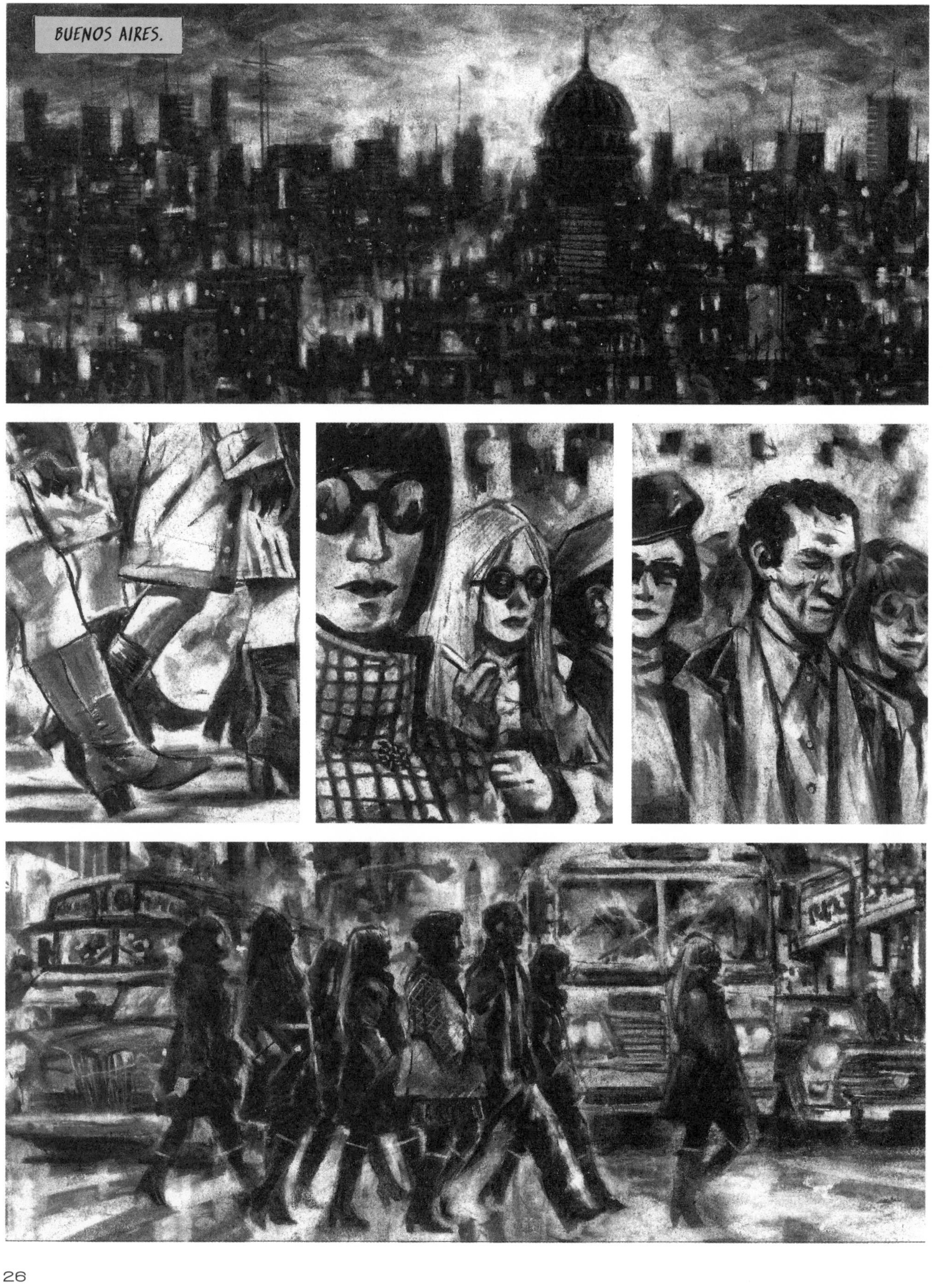
BUENOS AIRES.

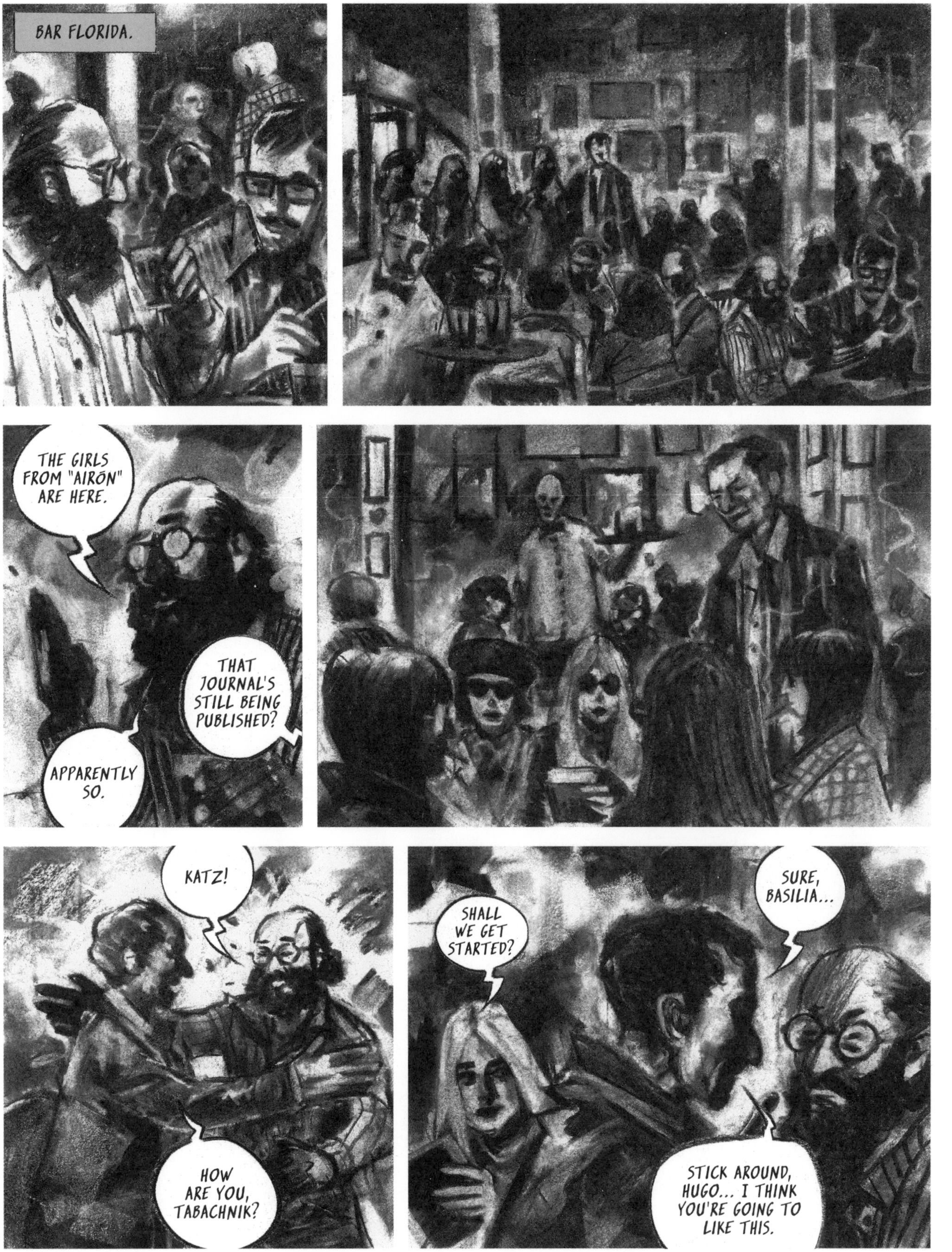
BAR FLORIDA.
THE GIRLS FROM "AIRÓN" ARE HERE.
THAT JOURNAL'S STILL BEING PUBLISHED?
APPARENTLY SO.
KATZ!
HOW ARE YOU, TABACHNIK?
SURE, BASILIA...
SHALL WE GET STARTED?
STICK AROUND, HUGO... I THINK YOU'RE GOING TO LIKE THIS.

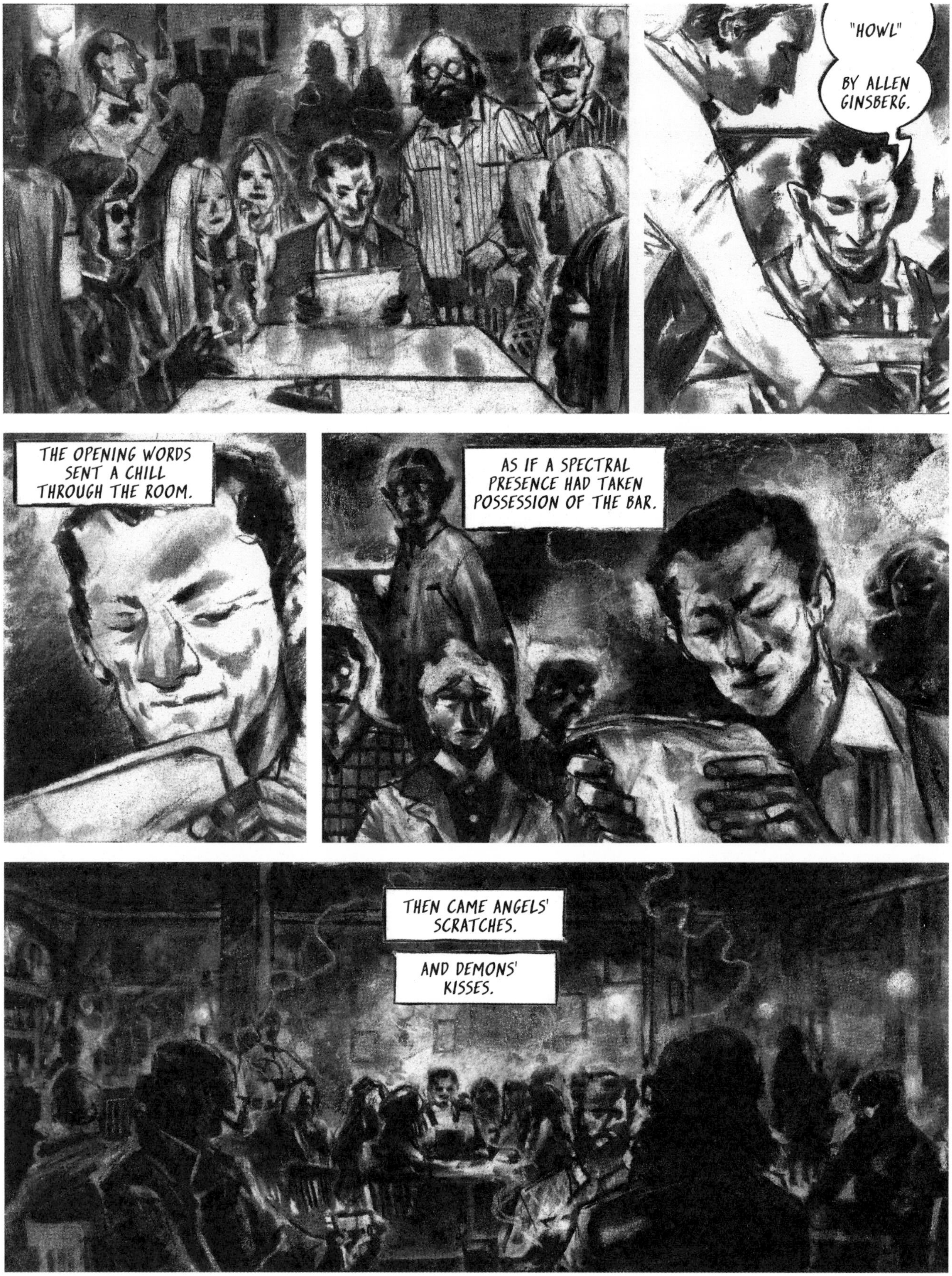
"HOWL"
BY ALLEN GINSBERG.
THE OPENING WORDS SENT A CHILL THROUGH THE ROOM.
AS IF A SPECTRAL PRESENCE HAD TAKEN POSSESSION OF THE BAR.
THEN CAME ANGELS' SCRATCHES.
AND DEMONS' KISSES.

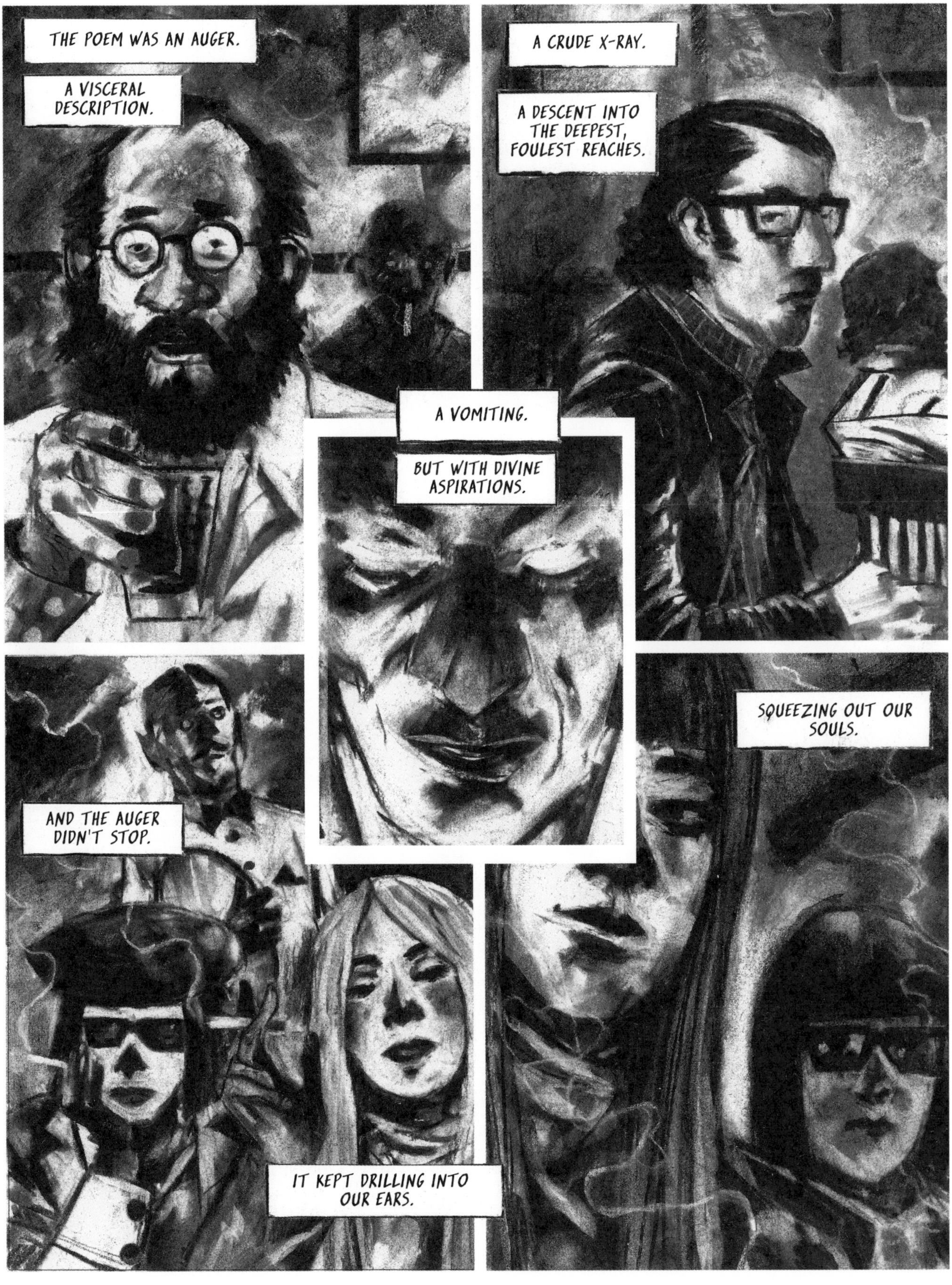
THE POEM WAS AN AUGER.
A VISCERAL DESCRIPTION.
A CRUDE X-RAY.
A DESCENT INTO THE DEEPEST, FOULEST REACHES.
A VOMITING.
BUT WITH DIVINE ASPIRATIONS.
AND THE AUGER DIDN'T STOP.
IT KEPT DRILLING INTO OUR EARS.
SQUEEZING OUT OUR SOULS.

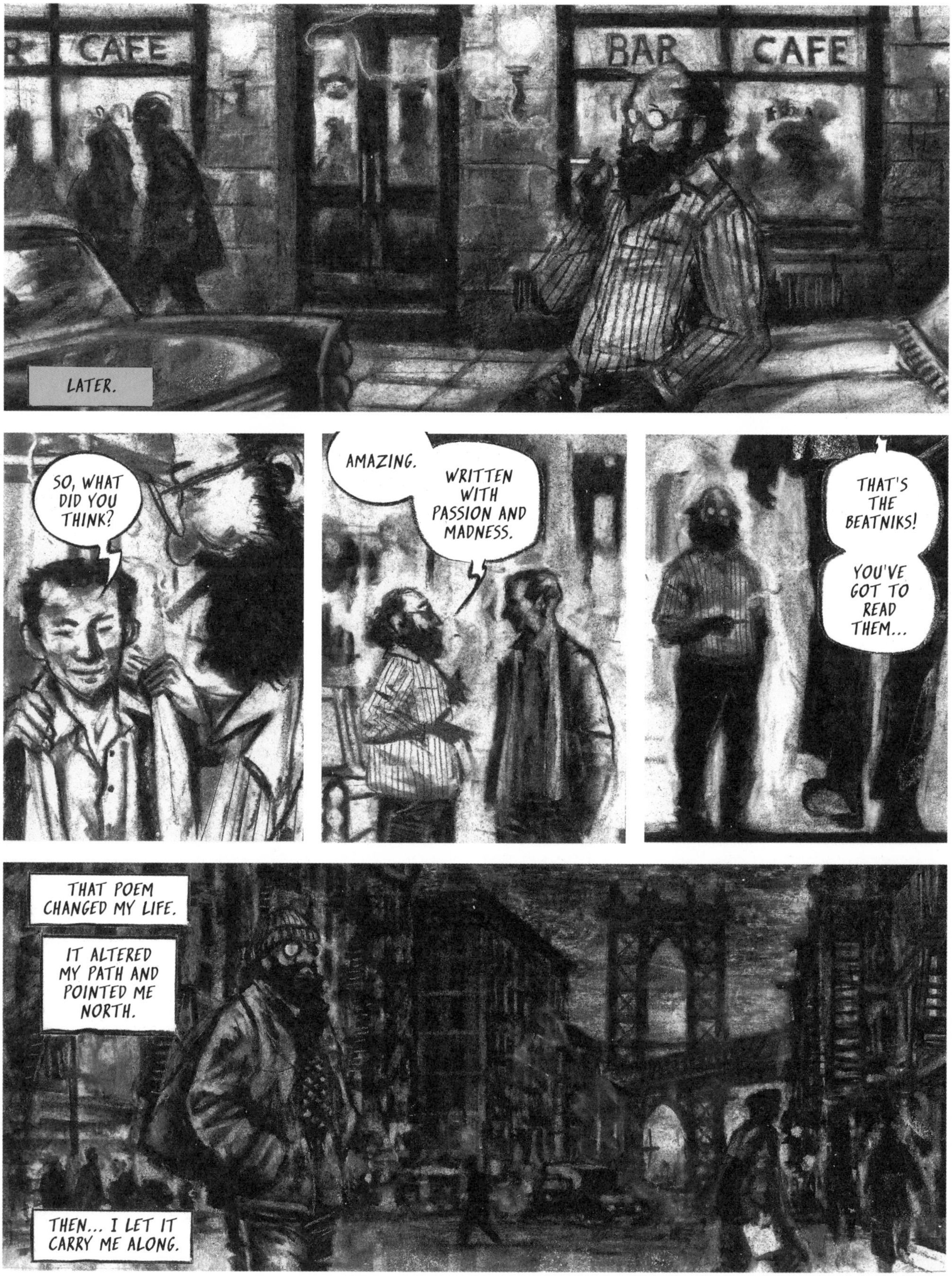
BAR
CAFE
LATER.
SO, WHAT DID YOU THINK?
AMAZING.
WRITTEN WITH PASSION AND MADNESS.
THAT'S THE BEATNIKS!
YOU'VE GOT TO READ THEM...
THAT POEM CHANGED MY LIFE.
IT ALTERED MY PATH AND POINTED ME NORTH.
THEN... I LET IT CARRY ME ALONG.

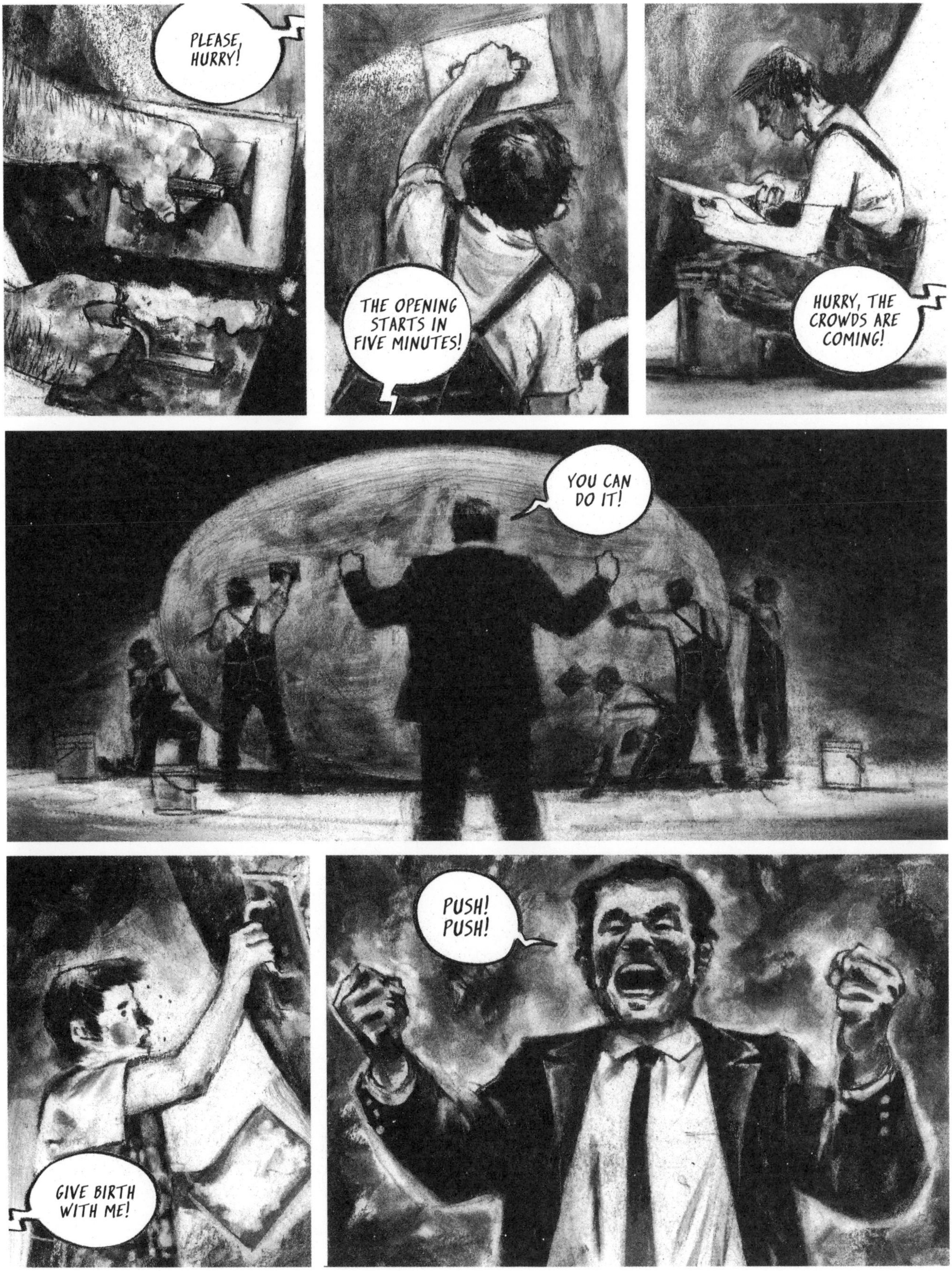
PLEASE, HURRY!
THE OPENING STARTS IN FIVE MINUTES!
HURRY, THE CROWDS ARE COMING!
YOU CAN DO IT!
GIVE BIRTH WITH ME!
PUSH! PUSH!

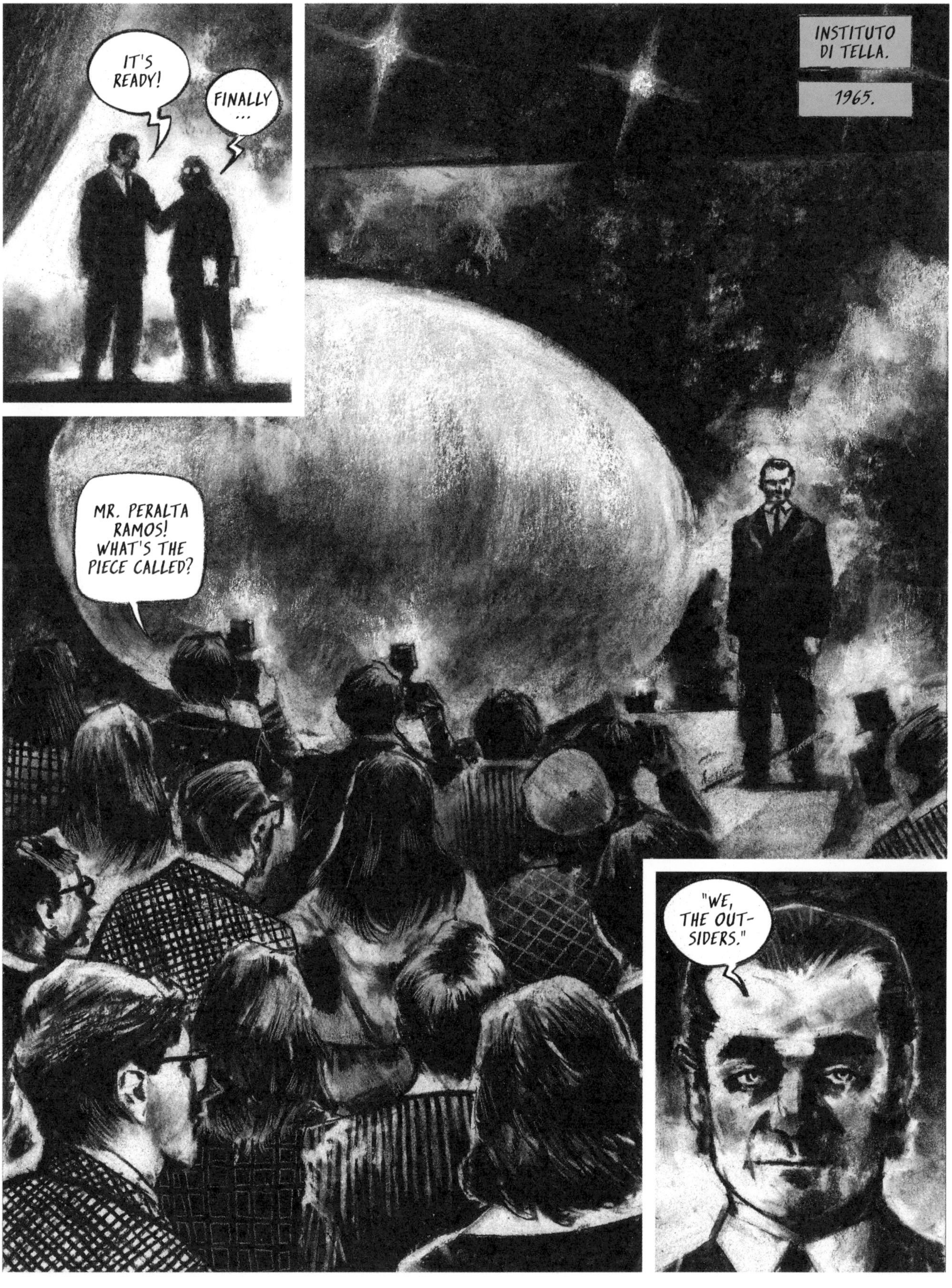
IT'S READY!
FINALLY ...
INSTITUTO DI TELLA.
1965.
MR. PERALTA RAMOS! WHAT'S THE PIECE CALLED?
"WE, THE OUT-SIDERS."

THREE YEARS LATER.

RiiiNG!

RiiiNG!

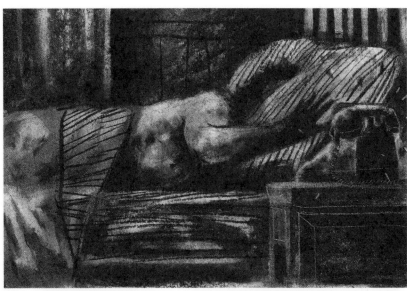

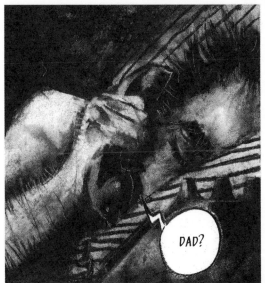

DAD?

NO, FEDERICO. THIS IS BAJARLÍA.

OH! HOW ARE YOU?

GOOD. I WANTED TO SEE IF WE COULD GET TOGETHER THIS AFTERNOON. IT'S FOR AN ARTICLE FOR THE PAPER.

I CAN'T DO THIS AFTER-NOON. TONIGHT WOULD WORK-- SAY, TEN?

HOW ABOUT AT BAR LA PAZ?

NO, NO! THE FLORIDA GARDEN!

SOUNDS GOOD. SEE YOU.

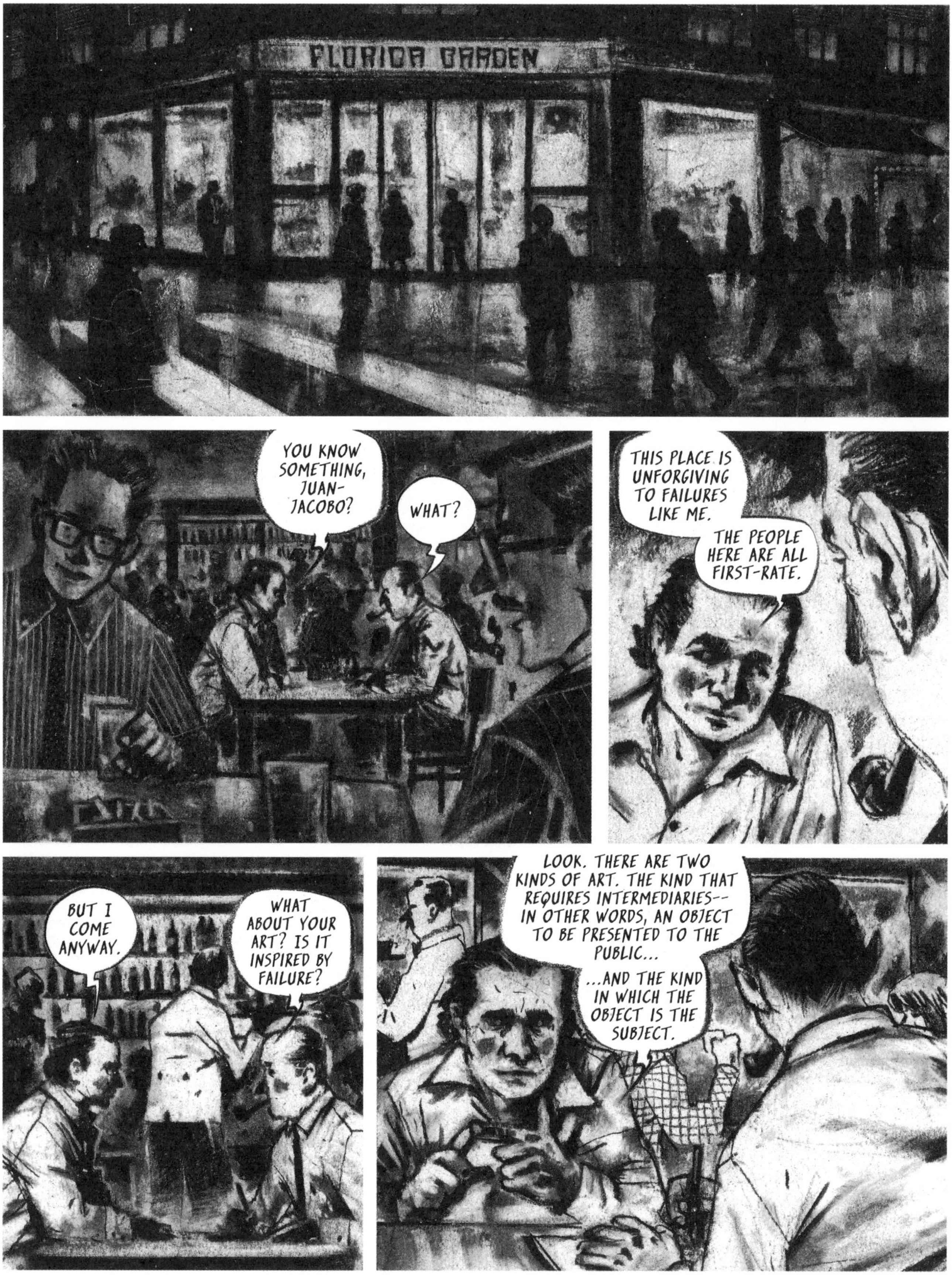
FLORIDA GARDEN
YOU KNOW SOMETHING, JUAN-JACOBO?
WHAT?
THIS PLACE IS UNFORGIVING TO FAILURES LIKE ME.
THE PEOPLE HERE ARE ALL FIRST-RATE.
BUT I COME ANYWAY.
WHAT ABOUT YOUR ART? IS IT INSPIRED BY FAILURE?
LOOK. THERE ARE TWO KINDS OF ART. THE KIND THAT REQUIRES INTERMEDIARIES--IN OTHER WORDS, AN OBJECT TO BE PRESENTED TO THE PUBLIC...
...AND THE KIND IN WHICH THE OBJECT IS THE SUBJECT.

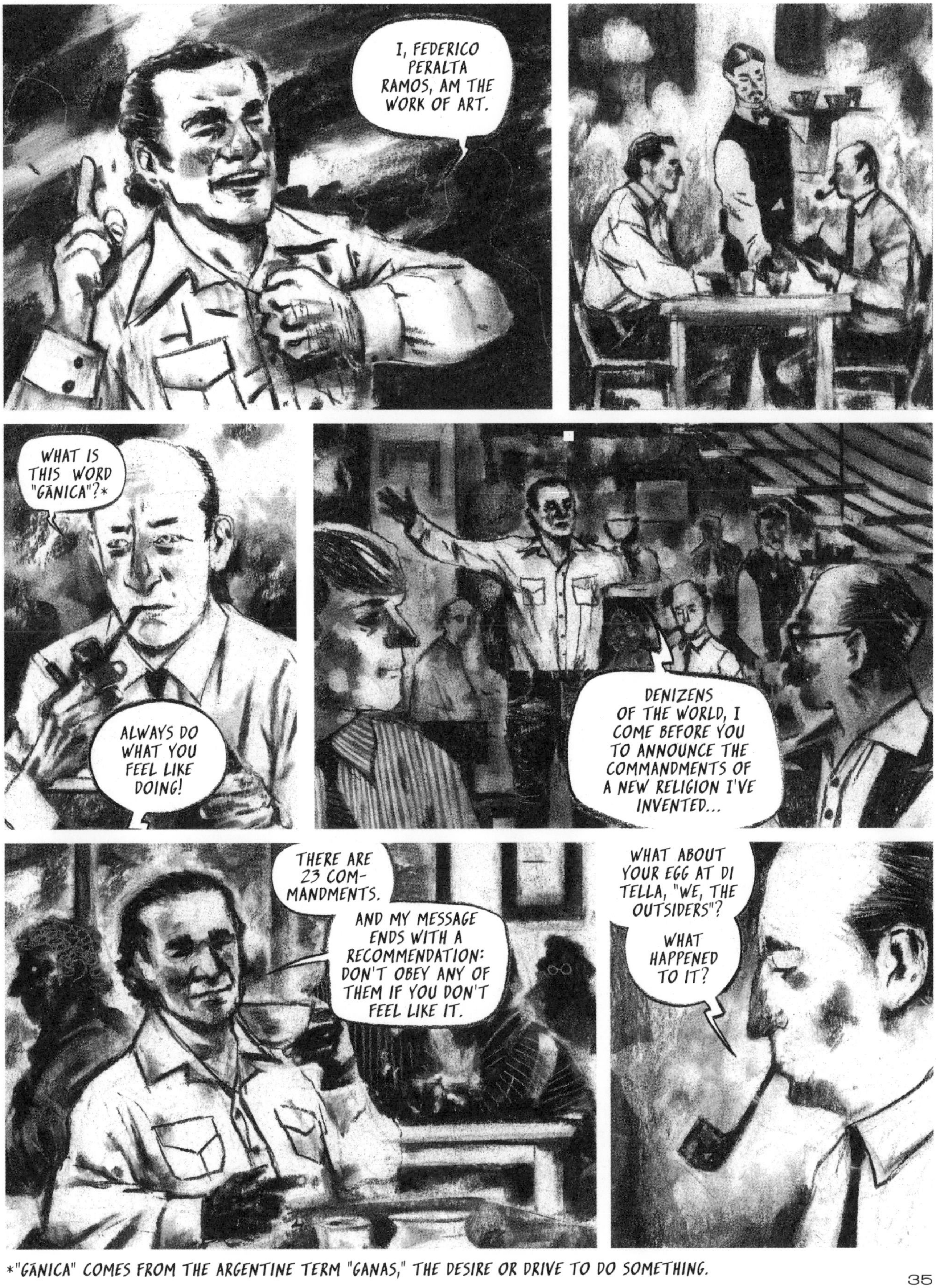
I, FEDERICO PERALTA RAMOS, AM THE WORK OF ART.
WHAT IS THIS WORD "GĀNICA"?*
ALWAYS DO WHAT YOU FEEL LIKE DOING!
DENIZENS OF THE WORLD, I COME BEFORE YOU TO ANNOUNCE THE COMMANDMENTS OF A NEW RELIGION I'VE INVENTED...
THERE ARE 23 COM-MANDMENTS.
AND MY MESSAGE ENDS WITH A RECOMMENDATION: DON'T OBEY ANY OF THEM IF YOU DON'T FEEL LIKE IT.
WHAT ABOUT YOUR EGG AT DI TELLA, "WE, THE OUTSIDERS"?
WHAT HAPPENED TO IT?

*"GĀNICA" COMES FROM THE ARGENTINE TERM "GANAS," THE DESIRE OR DRIVE TO DO SOMETHING.

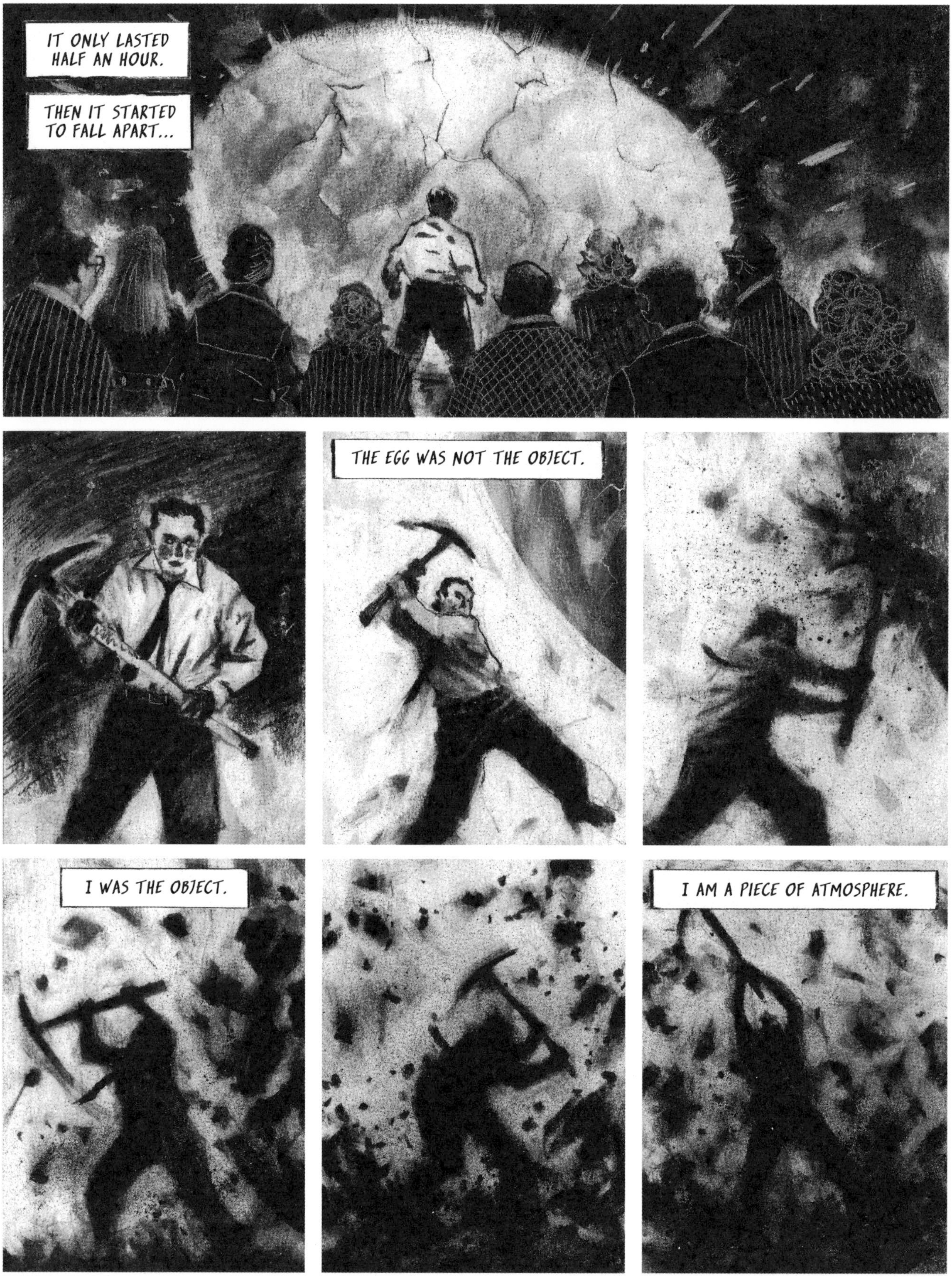
IT ONLY LASTED HALF AN HOUR.
THEN IT STARTED TO FALL APART...
THE EGG WAS NOT THE OBJECT.
I WAS THE OBJECT.
I AM A PIECE OF ATMOSPHERE.

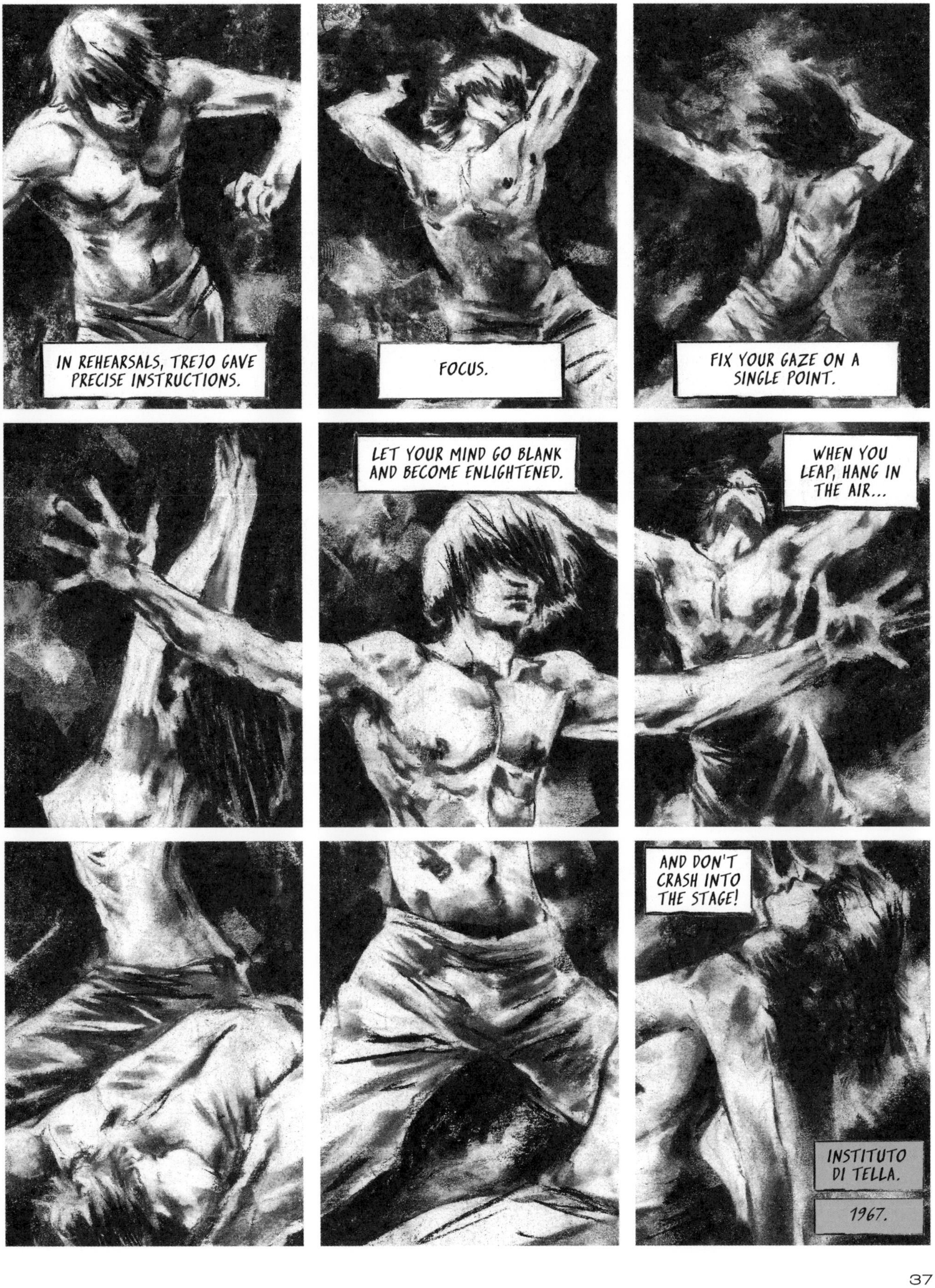
IN REHEARSALS, TREJO GAVE PRECISE INSTRUCTIONS.
FOCUS.
FIX YOUR GAZE ON A SINGLE POINT.
LET YOUR MIND GO BLANK AND BECOME ENLIGHTENED.
WHEN YOU LEAP, HANG IN THE AIR...
AND DON'T CRASH INTO THE STAGE!
INSTITUTO DI TELLA.
1967.

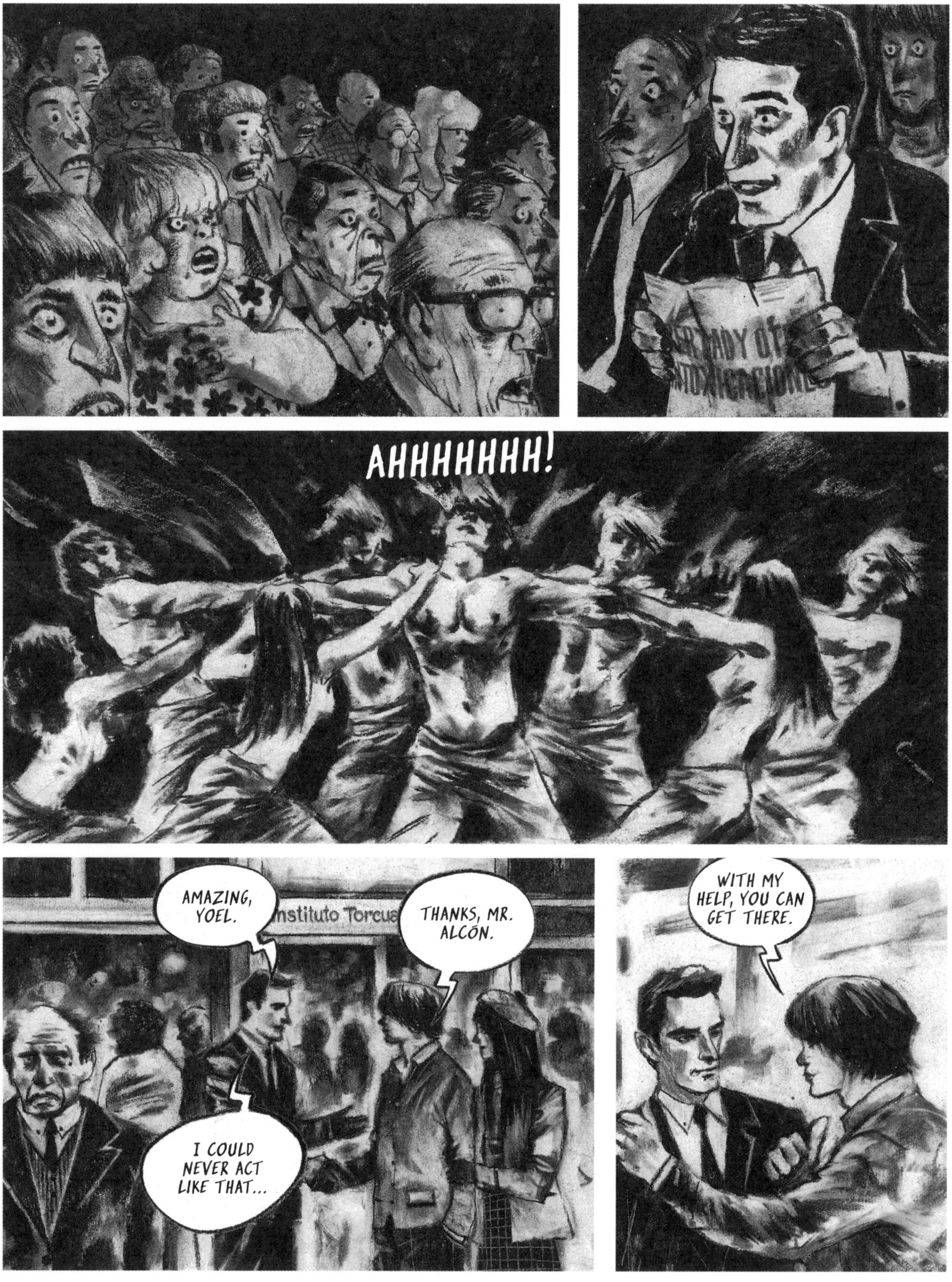
AHHHHHHH!
Instituto Torcua
AMAZING, YOEL.
I COULD NEVER ACT LIKE THAT...
THANKS, MR. ALCÓN.
WITH MY HELP, YOU CAN GET THERE.

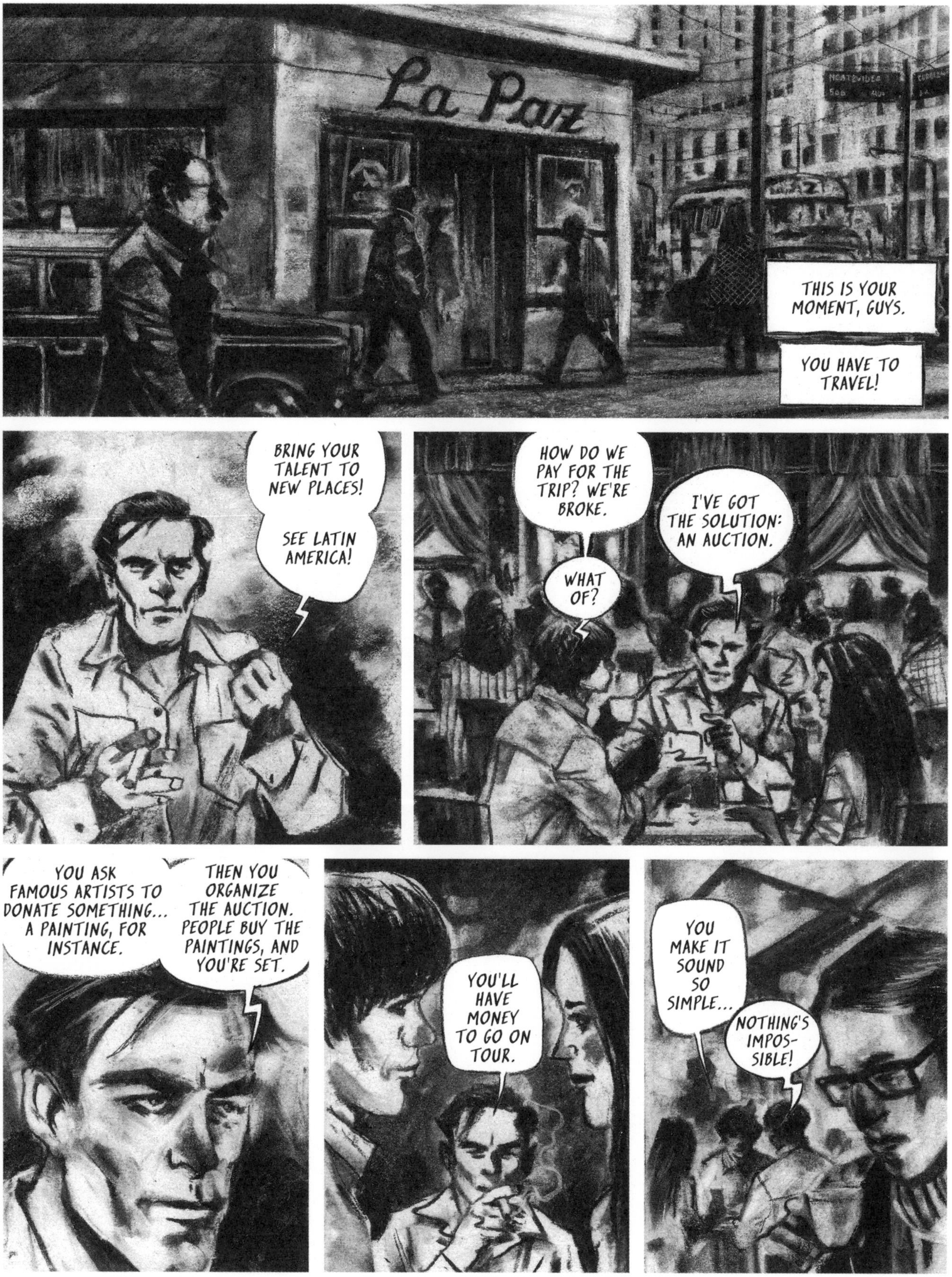
La Paz
THIS IS YOUR MOMENT, GUYS.
YOU HAVE TO TRAVEL!
BRING YOUR TALENT TO NEW PLACES!
SEE LATIN AMERICA!
HOW DO WE PAY FOR THE TRIP? WE'RE BROKE.
I'VE GOT THE SOLUTION: AN AUCTION.
WHAT OF?
YOU ASK FAMOUS ARTISTS TO DONATE SOMETHING... A PAINTING, FOR INSTANCE.
THEN YOU ORGANIZE THE AUCTION. PEOPLE BUY THE PAINTINGS, AND YOU'RE SET.
YOU'LL HAVE MONEY TO GO ON TOUR.
YOU MAKE IT SOUND SO SIMPLE...
NOTHING'S IMPOS-SIBLE!

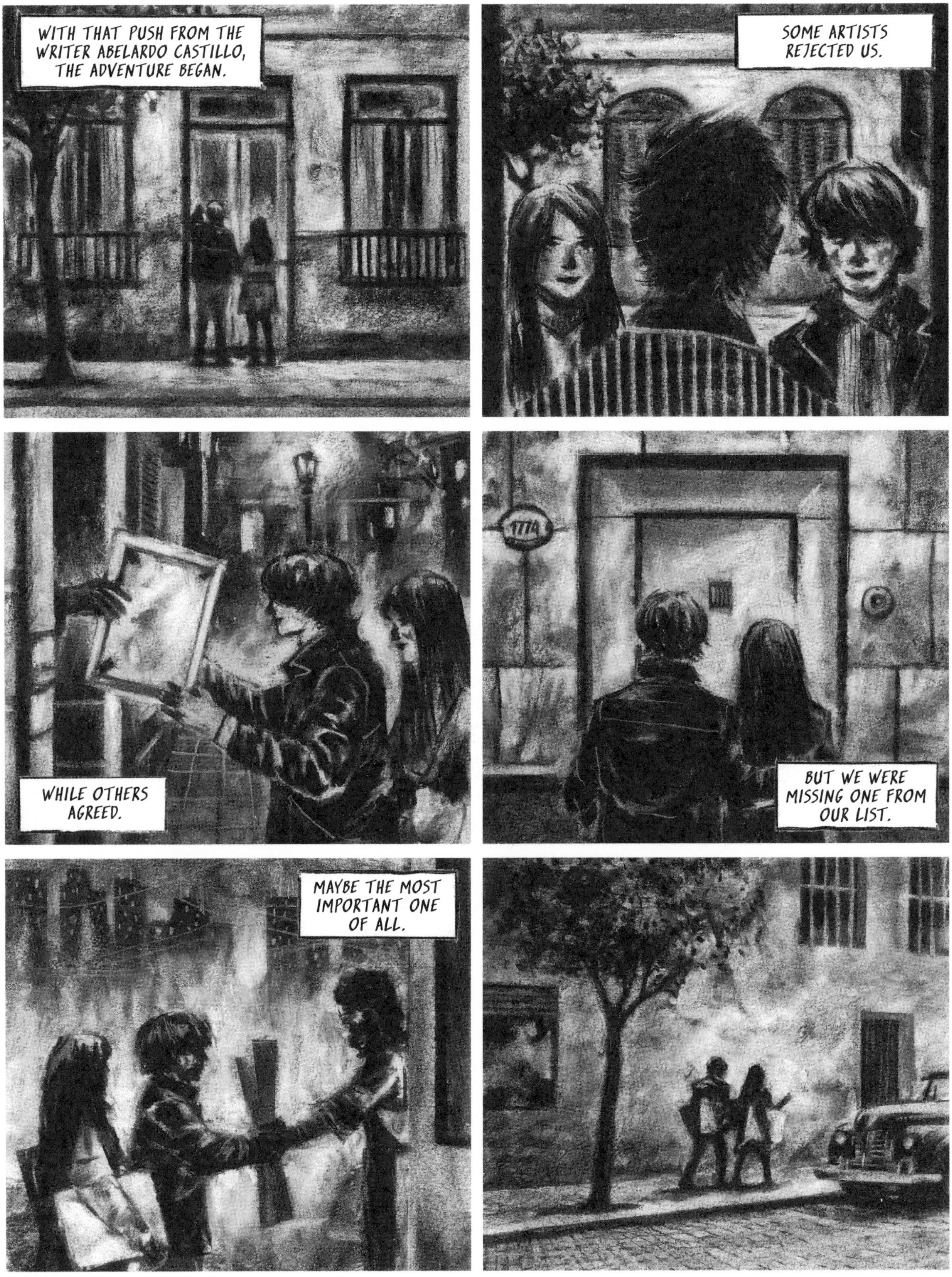
WITH THAT PUSH FROM THE WRITER ABELARDO CASTILLO, THE ADVENTURE BEGAN.
SOME ARTISTS REJECTED US.
WHILE OTHERS AGREED.
1774
BUT WE WERE MISSING ONE FROM OUR LIST.
MAYBE THE MOST IMPORTANT ONE OF ALL.

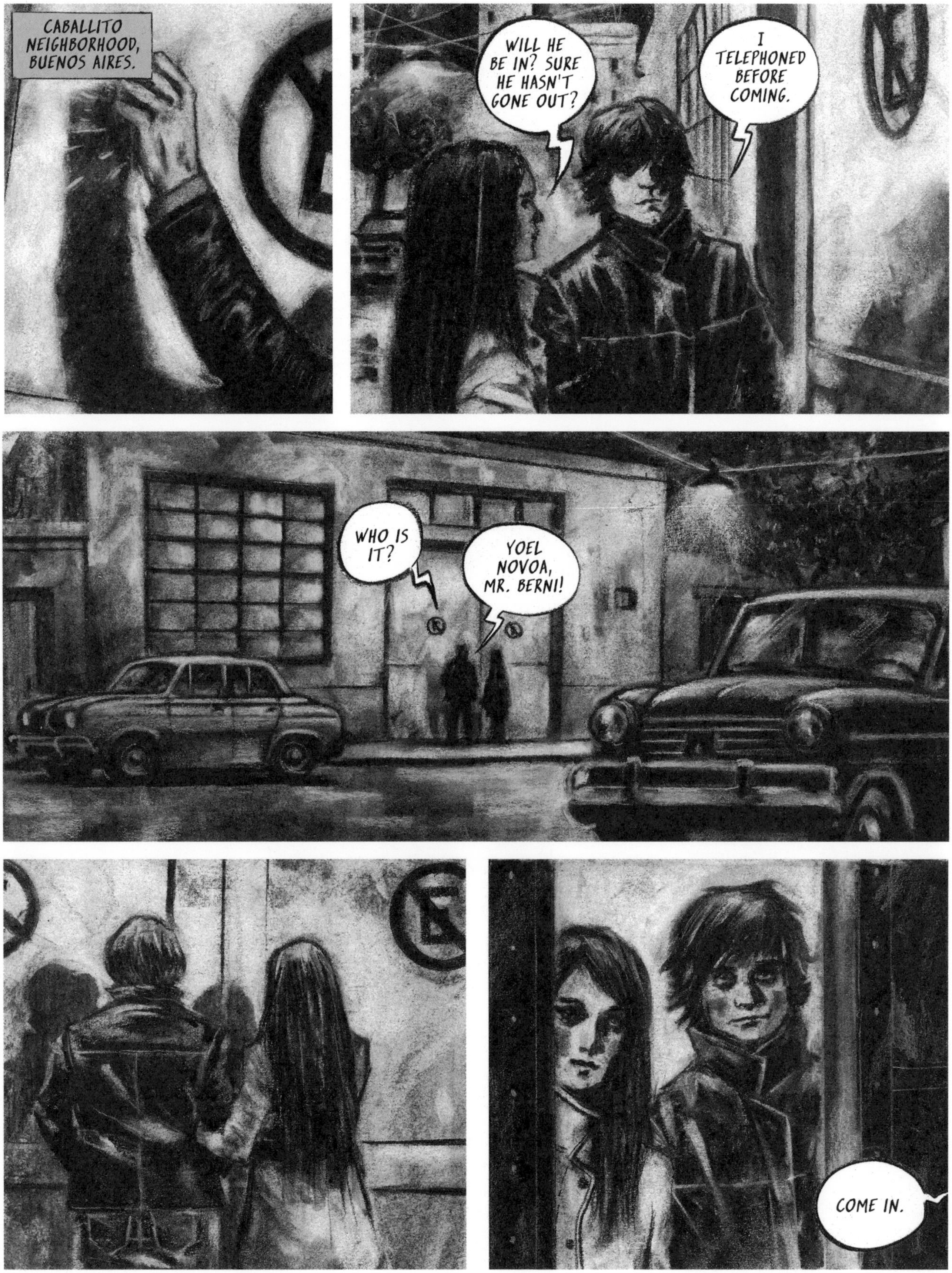
CABALLITO NEIGHBORHOOD, BUENOS AIRES.
WILL HE BE IN? SURE HE HASN'T GONE OUT?
I TELEPHONED BEFORE COMING.
WHO IS IT?
YOEL NOVOA, MR. BERNI!
COME IN.

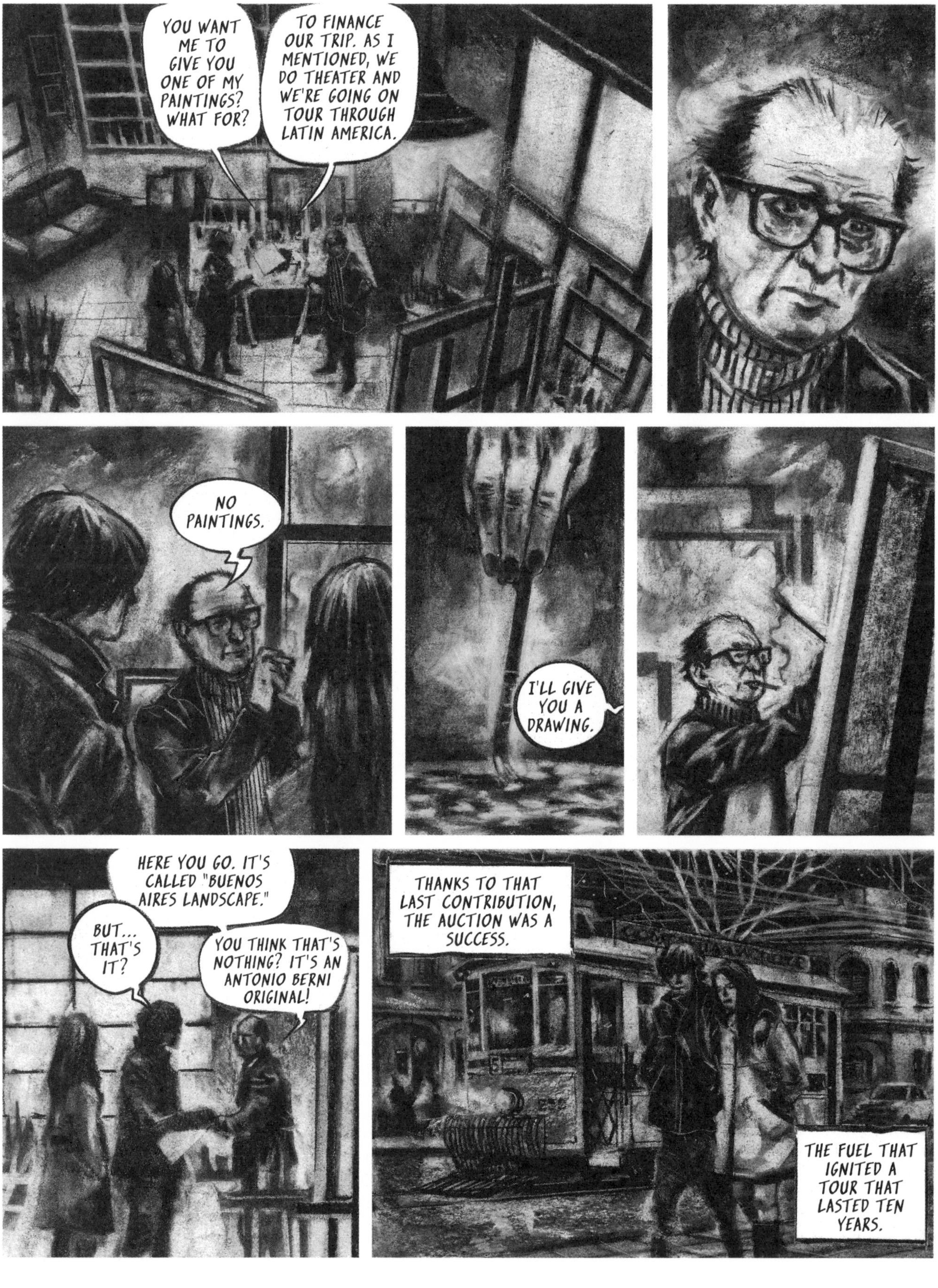
YOU WANT ME TO GIVE YOU ONE OF MY PAINTINGS? WHAT FOR?
TO FINANCE OUR TRIP. AS I MENTIONED, WE DO THEATER AND WE'RE GOING ON TOUR THROUGH LATIN AMERICA.
NO PAINTINGS.
I'LL GIVE YOU A DRAWING.
HERE YOU GO. IT'S CALLED "BUENOS AIRES LANDSCAPE."
BUT... THAT'S IT?
YOU THINK THAT'S NOTHING? IT'S AN ANTONIO BERNI ORIGINAL!
THANKS TO THAT LAST CONTRIBUTION, THE AUCTION WAS A SUCCESS.
THE FUEL THAT IGNITED A TOUR THAT LASTED TEN YEARS.

IT'S USELESS.

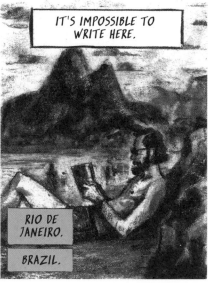

IT'S IMPOSSIBLE TO WRITE HERE.

RIO DE JANEIRO.

BRAZIL.

ALL YOU CAN DO IS READ. READ TILL YOUR EYES EXPLODE.

TUMP!

GOD-DAMMIT!

SORRY, MISTER! THE BALL!

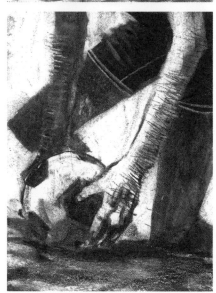

HERE YOU GO!

AND LIVE.

YOU MUSTN'T EVER FORGET TO LIVE.

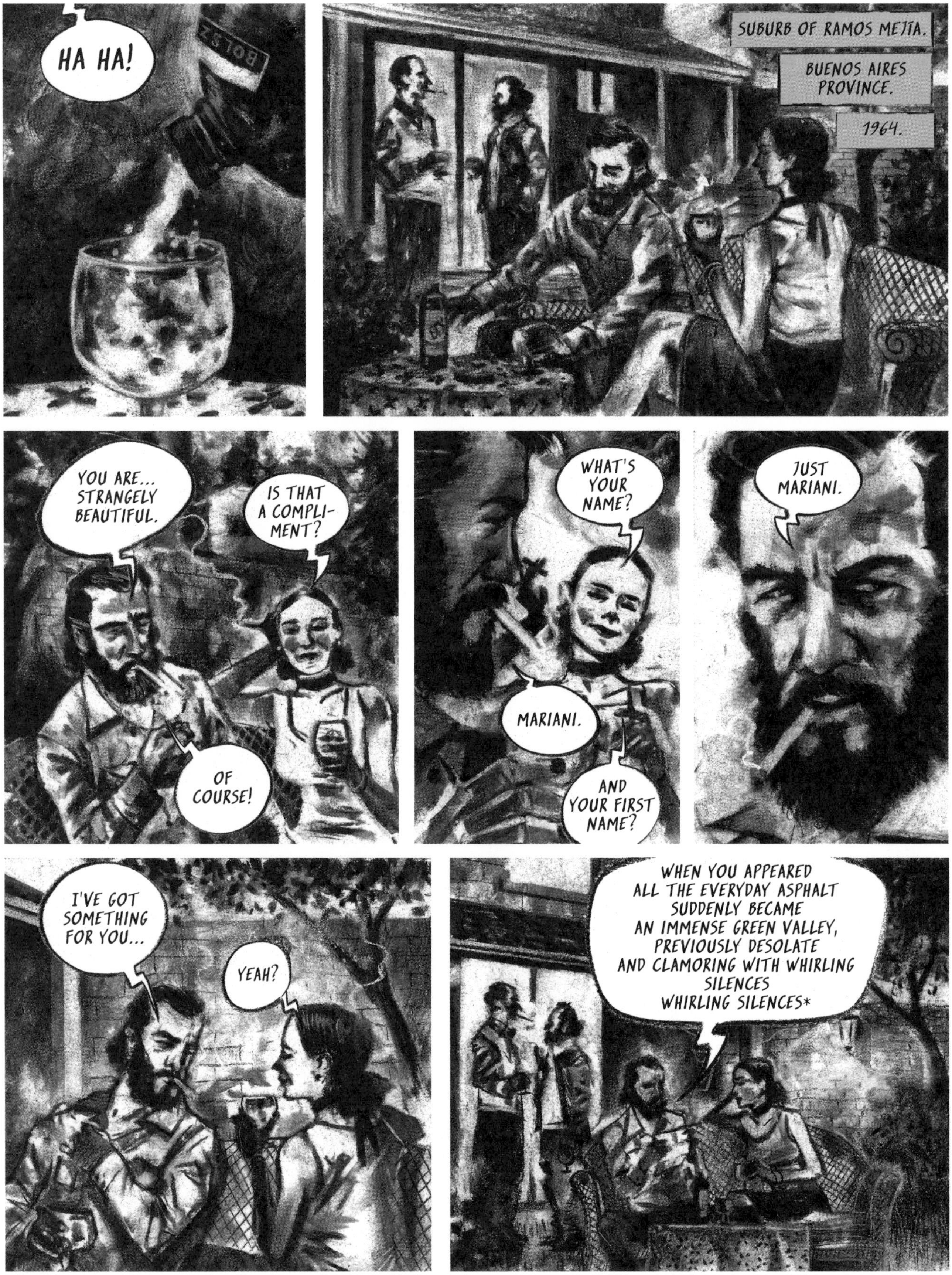
HA HA!
SUBURB OF RAMOS MEJIA.
BUENOS AIRES PROVINCE.
1964.
YOU ARE... STRANGELY BEAUTIFUL.
IS THAT A COMPLI- MENT?
OF COURSE!
WHAT'S YOUR NAME?
MARIANI.
AND YOUR FIRST NAME?
JUST MARIANI.
I'VE GOT SOMETHING FOR YOU...
YEAH?
WHEN YOU APPEARED
ALL THE EVERYDAY ASPHALT
SUDDENLY BECAME
AN IMMENSE GREEN VALLEY,
PREVIOUSLY DESOLATE
AND CLAMORING WITH WHIRLING
SILENCES
WHIRLING SILENCES*

*FROM "HISTORIA REPETIDA" ("HISTORY REPEATED") BY MARIANI

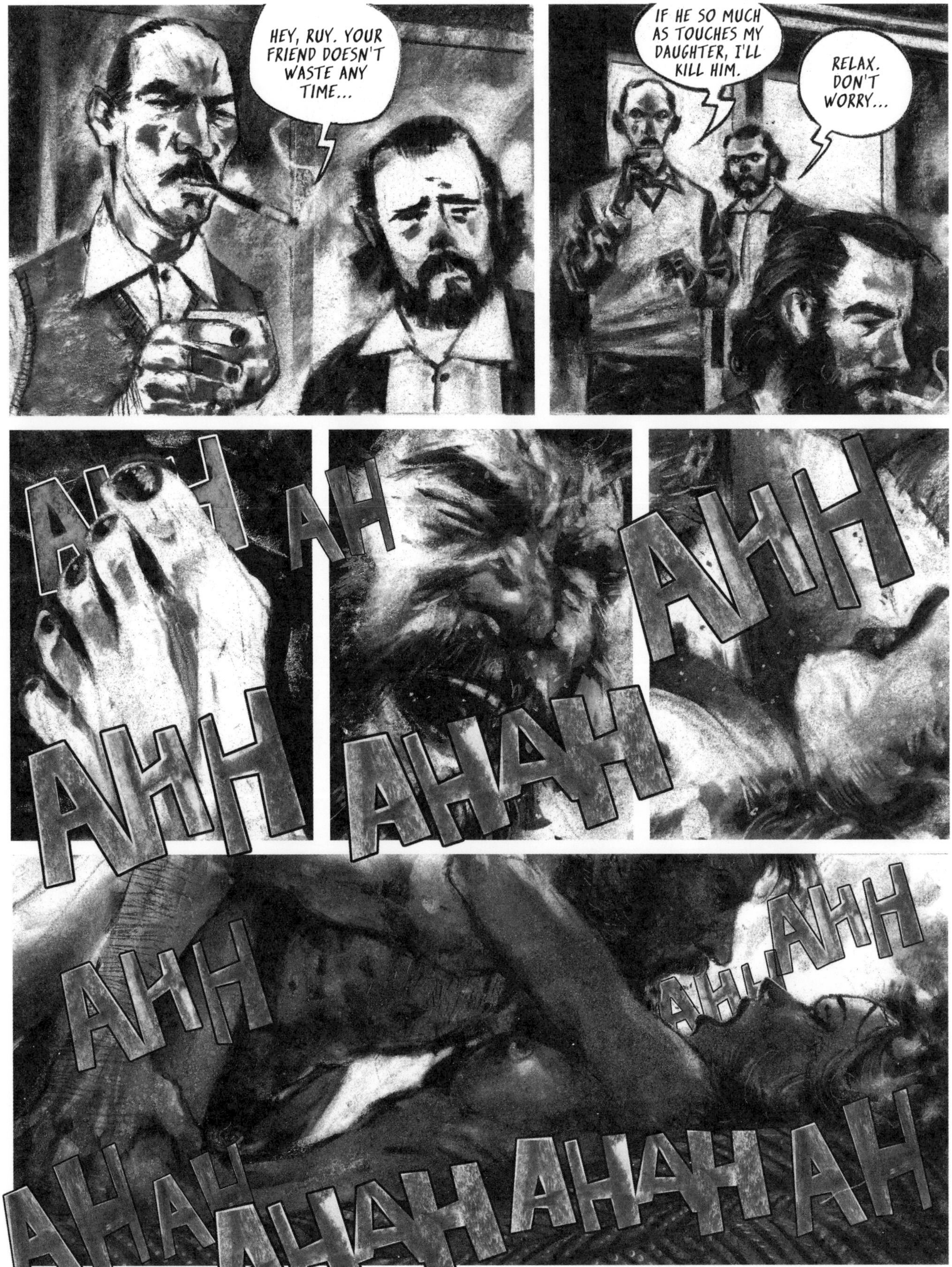
HEY, RUY. YOUR FRIEND DOESN'T WASTE ANY TIME...
IF HE SO MUCH AS TOUCHES MY DAUGHTER, I'LL KILL HIM.
RELAX. DON'T WORRY...
AHH
AH
AHH
AHH
AHAH
AHH
AHH
AHH
AHAH
AHAH
AHAH
AH

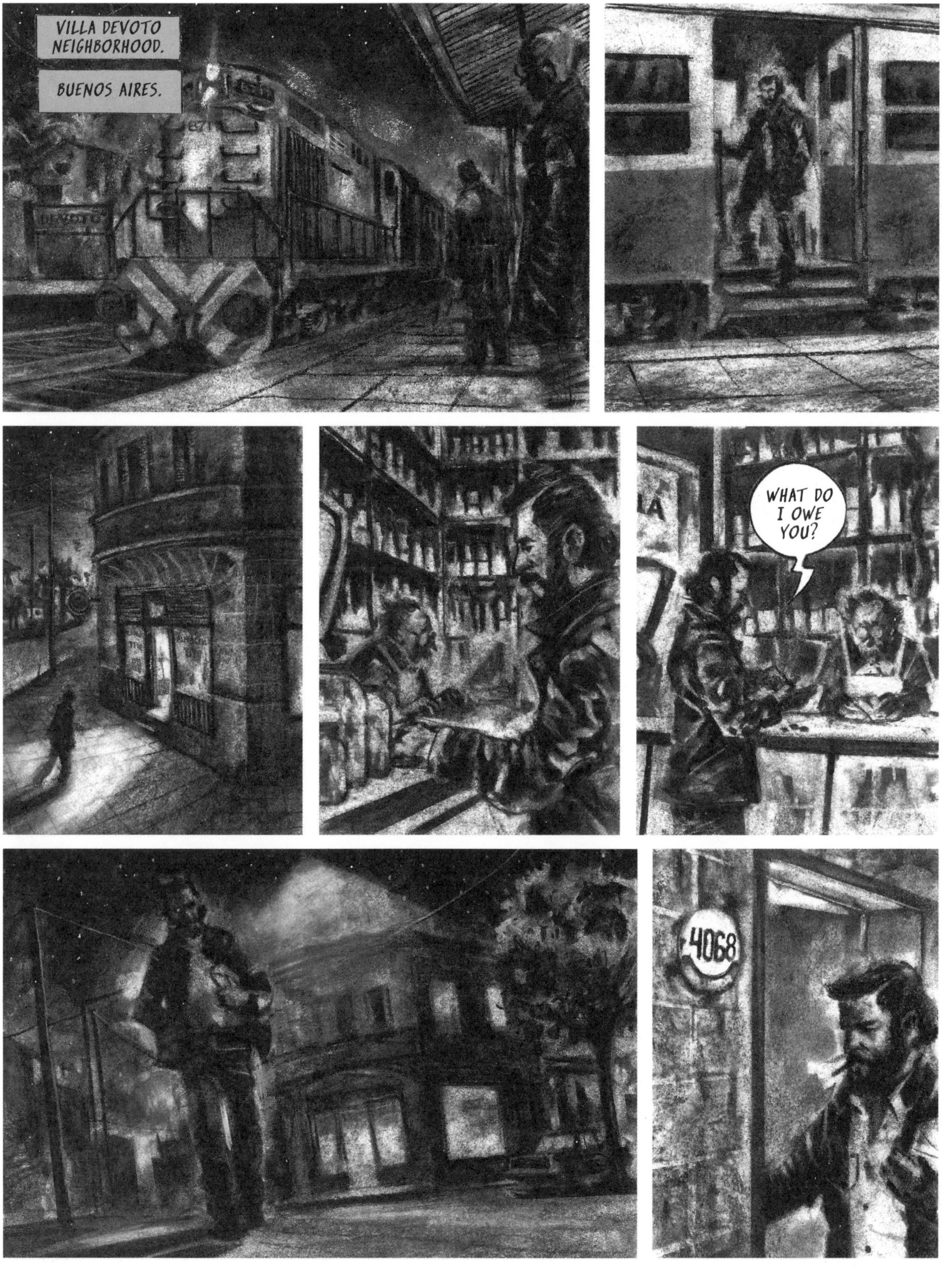
VILLA DEVOTO NEIGHBORHOOD.
BUENOS AIRES.
WHAT DO I OWE YOU?
4068

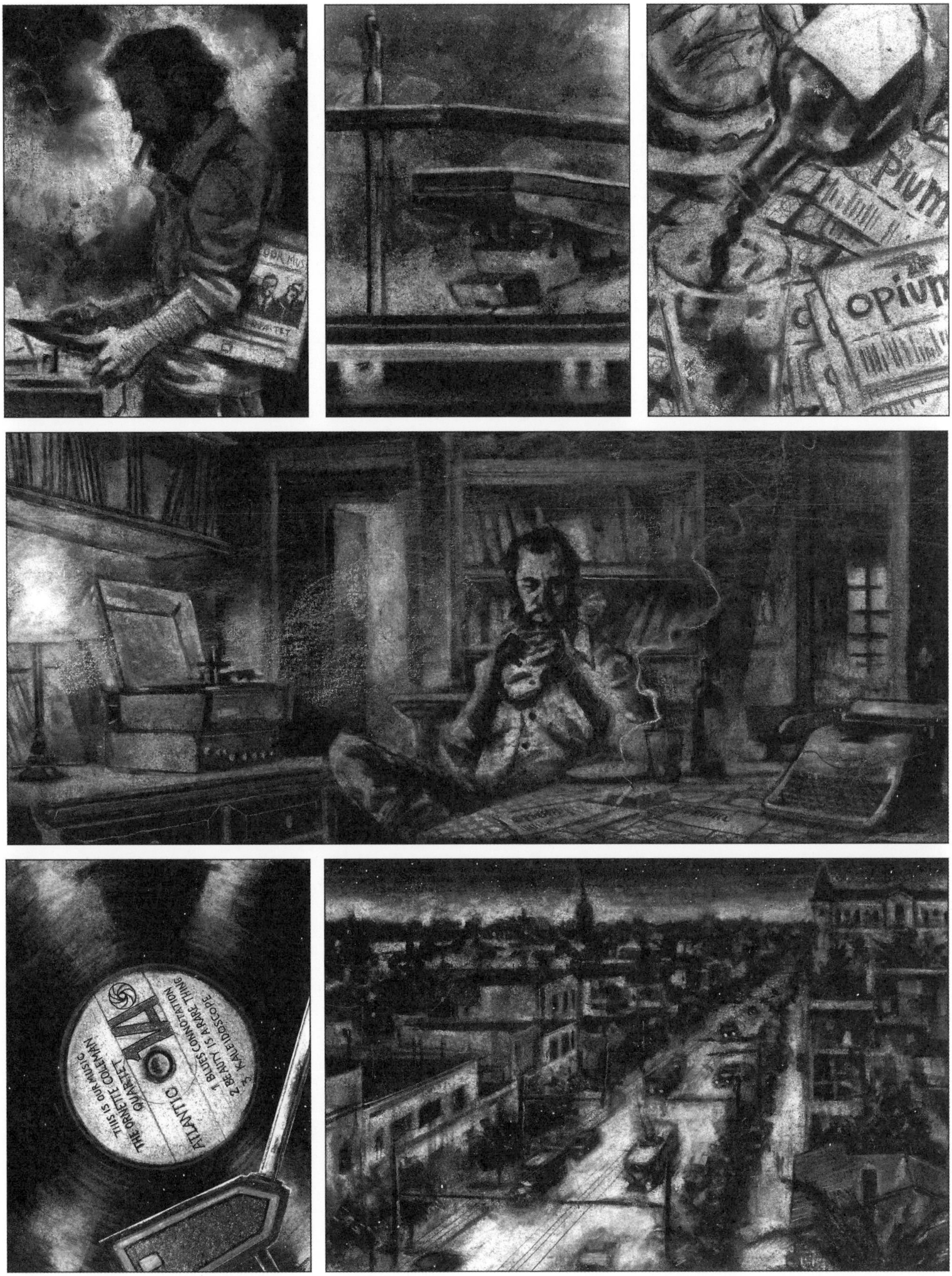
opium
THIS IS OUR MUSIC
THE ORNETTE COLEMAN QUARTET
ATLANTIC
1 BLUES CONNOTATION
2 BEAUTY IS A RARE THING
3 KALEIDOSCOPE

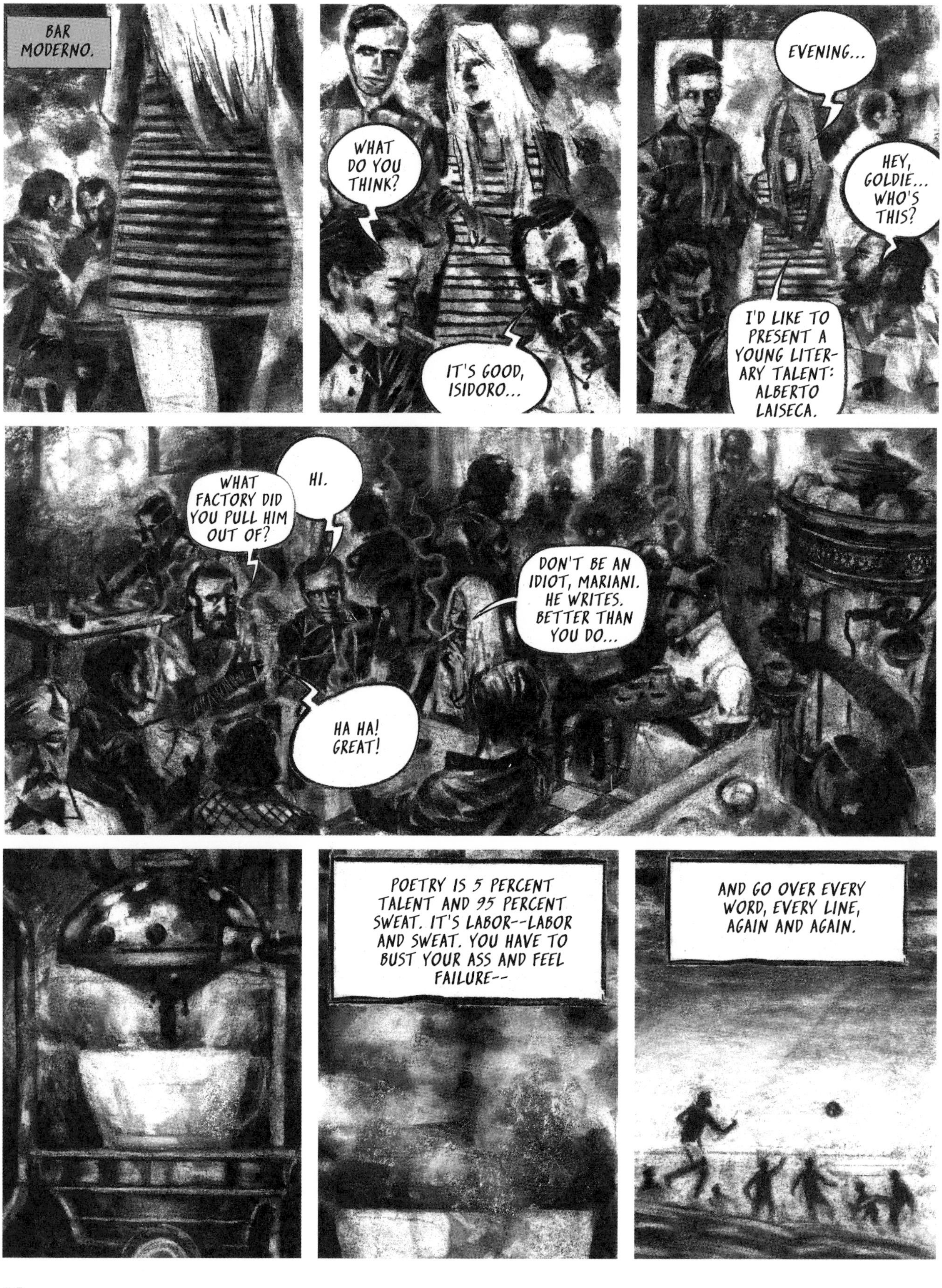
BAR MODERNO.
WHAT DO YOU THINK?
IT'S GOOD, ISIDORO...
EVENING...
HEY, GOLDIE... WHO'S THIS?
I'D LIKE TO PRESENT A YOUNG LITERARY TALENT: ALBERTO LAISECA.
HI.
WHAT FACTORY DID YOU PULL HIM OUT OF?
DON'T BE AN IDIOT, MARIANI. HE WRITES. BETTER THAN YOU DO...
HA HA! GREAT!
POETRY IS 5 PERCENT TALENT AND 95 PERCENT SWEAT. IT'S LABOR--LABOR AND SWEAT. YOU HAVE TO BUST YOUR ASS AND FEEL FAILURE--
AND GO OVER EVERY WORD, EVERY LINE, AGAIN AND AGAIN.

HERE, TIME DOESN'T EXIST.

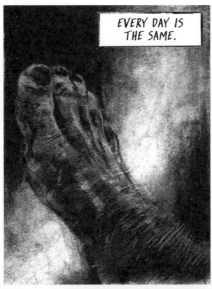

EVERY DAY IS THE SAME.

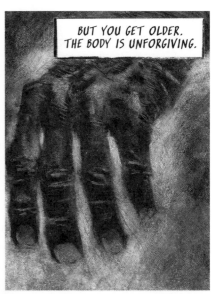

BUT YOU GET OLDER. THE BODY IS UNFORGIVING.

BOLIVIA.

IN PRISON, LIGHT IS A PRIVILEGE.

YOU END UP GETTING USED TO DARKNESS.

ULTIMATELY, YOU REALIZE YOU'VE GOT JUST ONE THING LEFT--POETRY.

SWEET DELIRIUM TO BELIEVE IN BESTIAL BLOOD SWEET IS THE STREET, THE FRUIT, THE VENGEANCE

THEY WON'T WANT TO DIE, THEY WON'T KNOW HOW WE'LL HAVE TO BLINDFOLD THEM

WE'LL HAVE TO GO TO THEIR HOUSES, DRAG THEM OUT LIKE HEADLESS CHICKENS*

*FROM "POEMA IV" ("POEM IV") BY SERGIO MULET

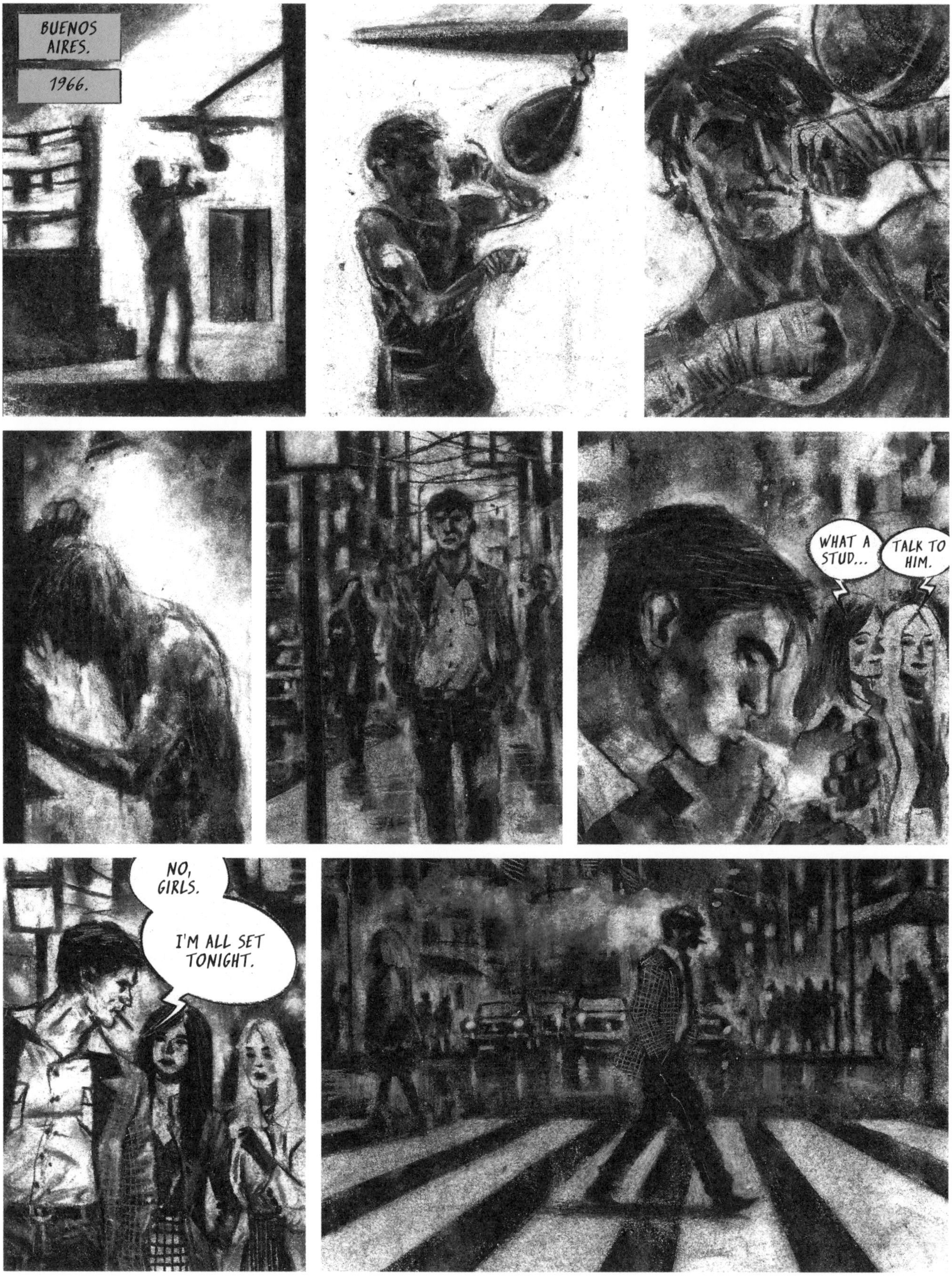
BUENOS AIRES.
1966.
WHAT A STUD...
TALK TO HIM.
NO, GIRLS.
I'M ALL SET TONIGHT.

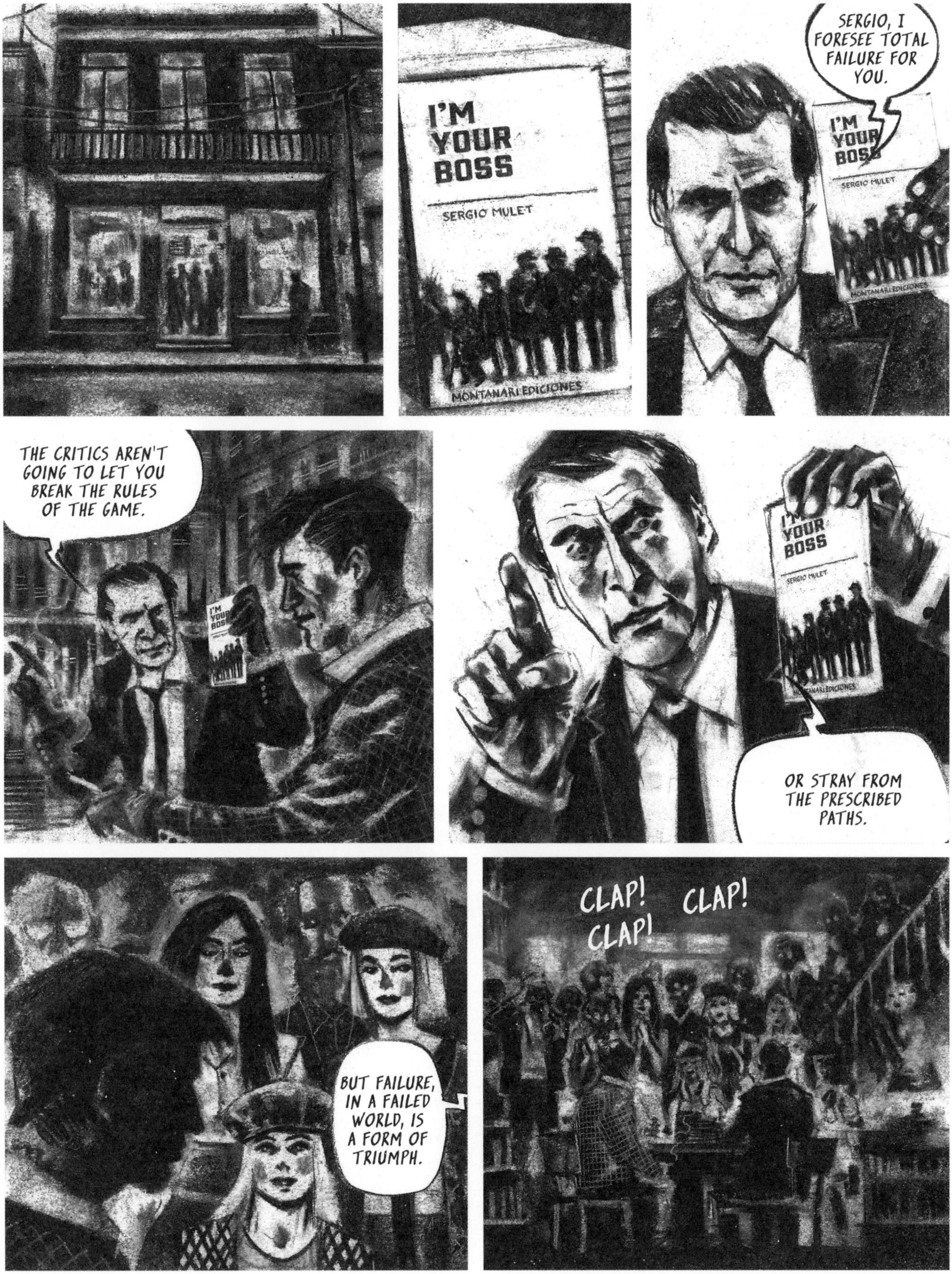
I'M YOUR BOSS
SERGIO MULET
MONTANARI EDICIONES
SERGIO, I FORESEE TOTAL FAILURE FOR YOU.
THE CRITICS AREN'T GOING TO LET YOU BREAK THE RULES OF THE GAME.
OR STRAY FROM THE PRESCRIBED PATHS.
BUT FAILURE, IN A FAILED WORLD, IS A FORM OF TRIUMPH.
CLAP! CLAP! CLAP!

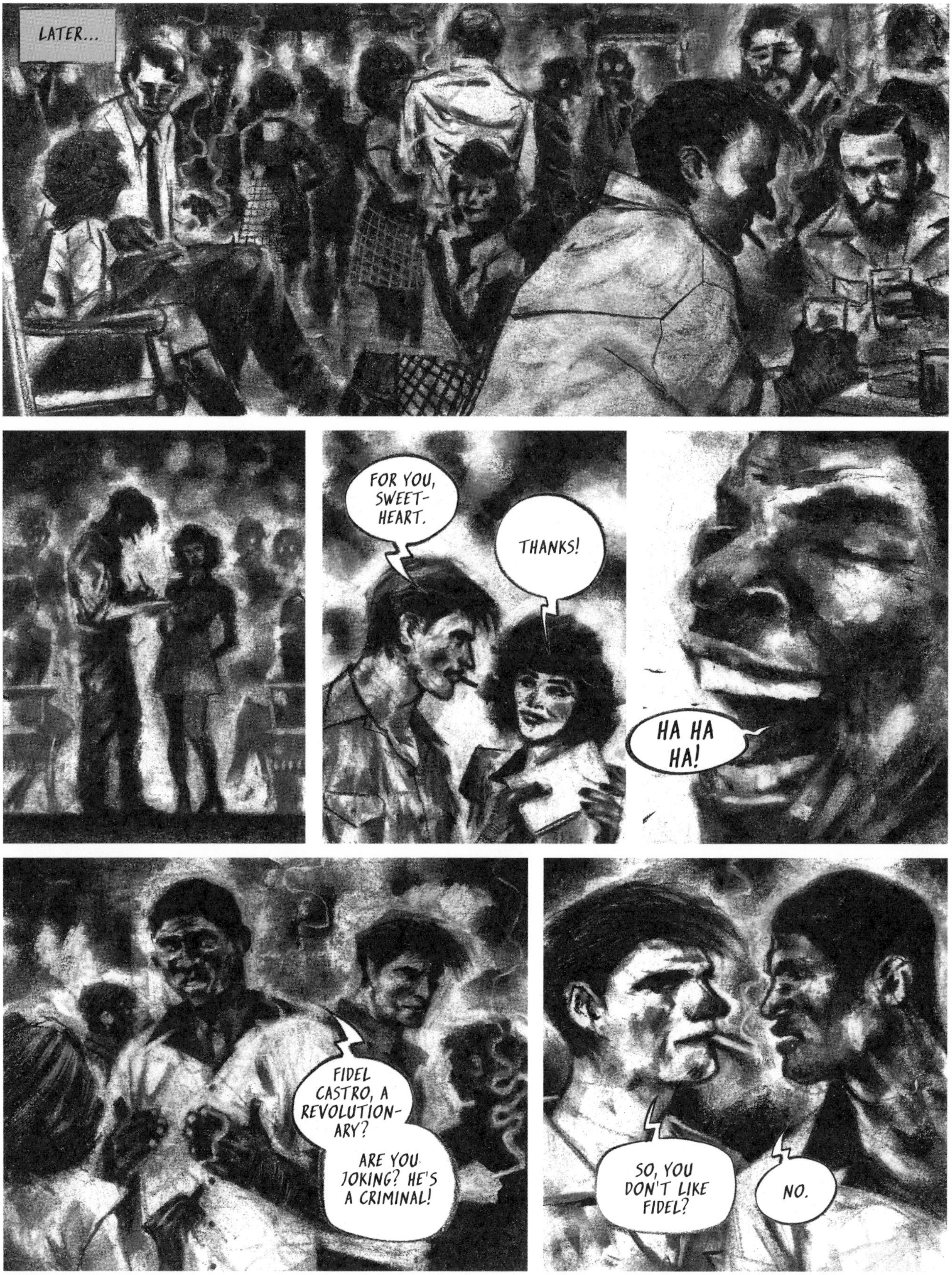
LATER...
FOR YOU, SWEET-HEART.
THANKS!
HA HA HA!
FIDEL CASTRO, A REVOLUTION-ARY?
ARE YOU JOKING? HE'S A CRIMINAL!
SO, YOU DON'T LIKE FIDEL?
NO.

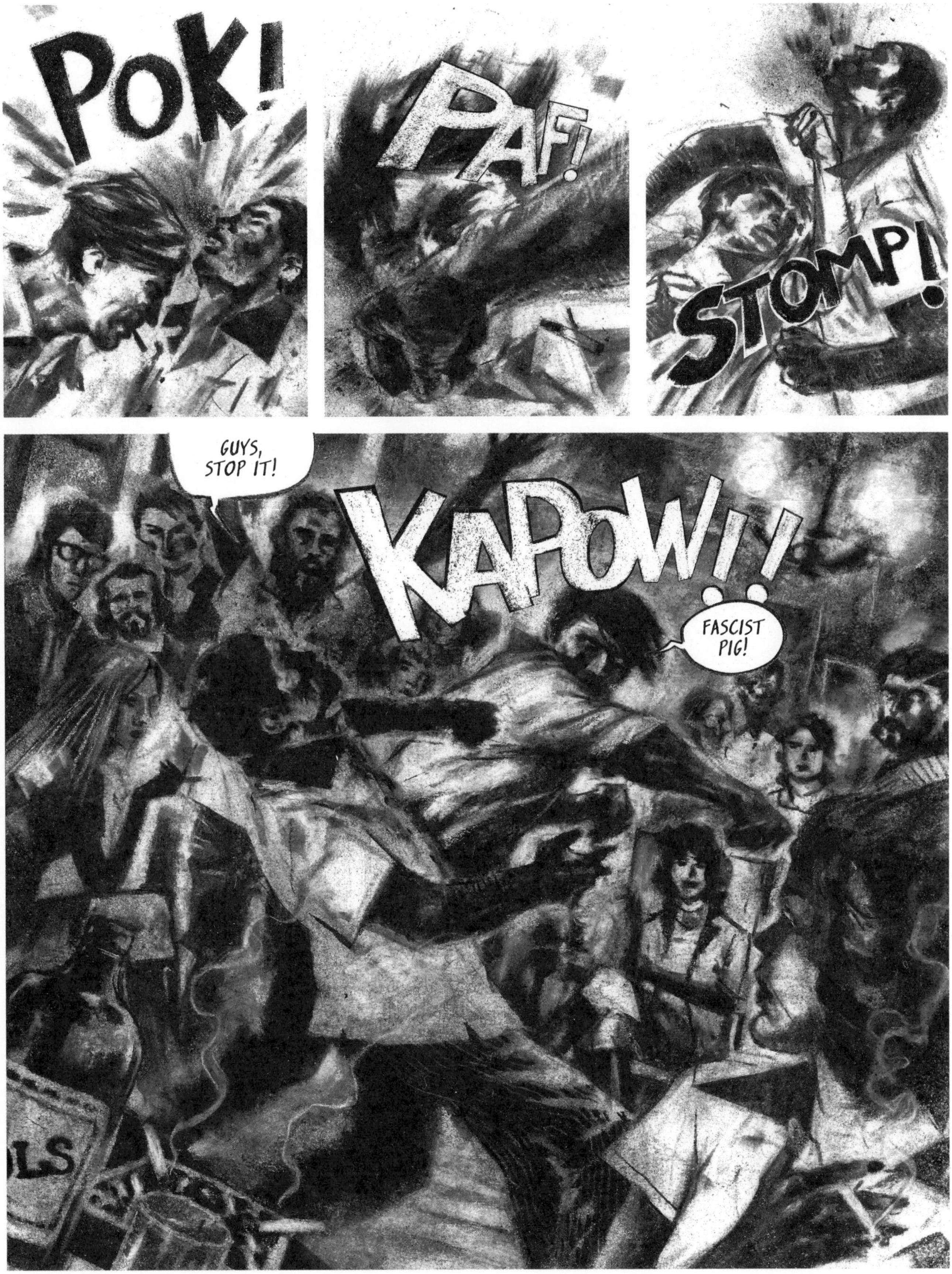
POK!
PAF!
STOMP!
GUYS, STOP IT!
KAPOW!!
FASCIST PIG!

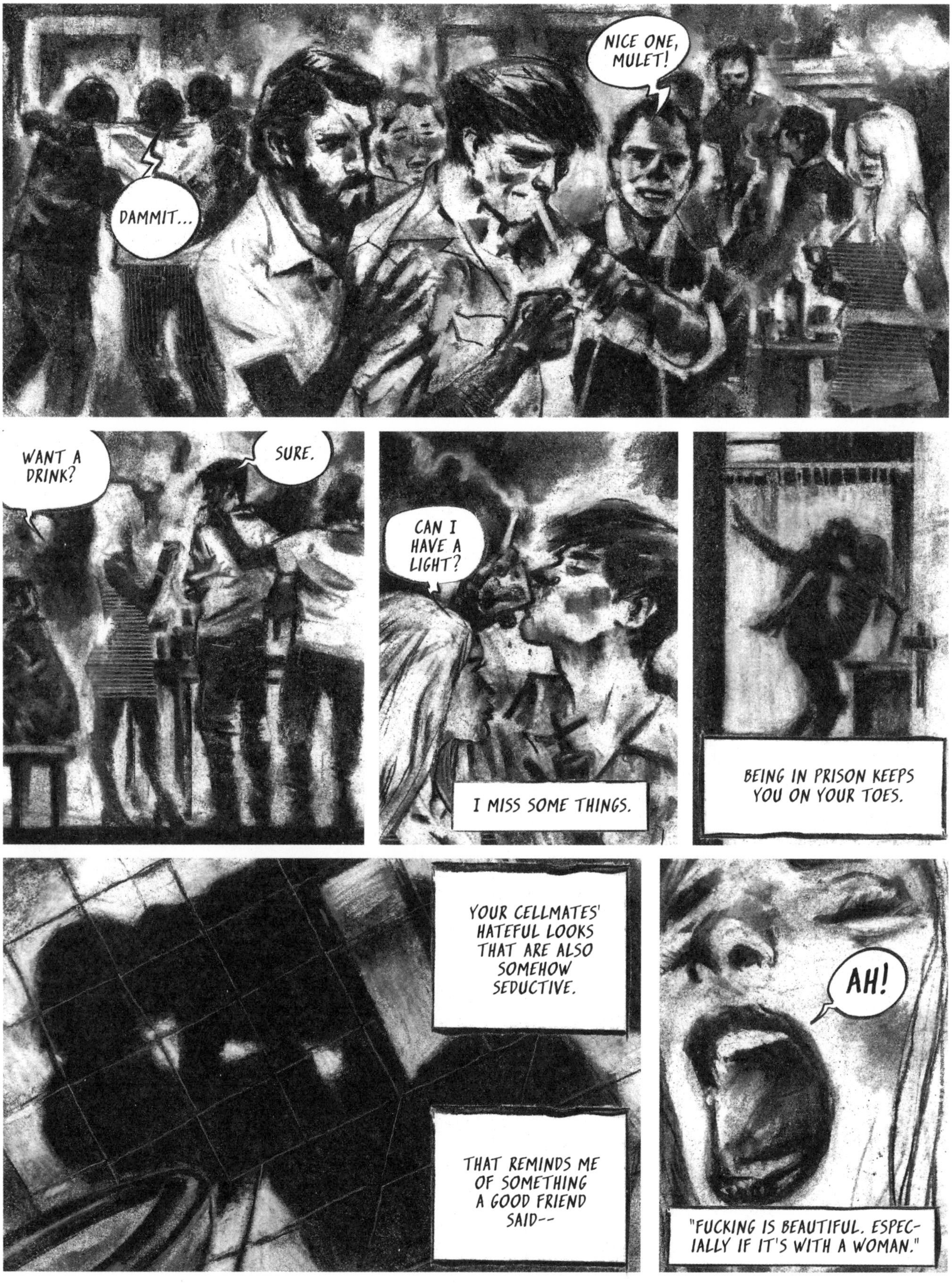
NICE ONE, MULET!
DAMMIT...
WANT A DRINK?
SURE.
CAN I HAVE A LIGHT?
I MISS SOME THINGS.
BEING IN PRISON KEEPS YOU ON YOUR TOES.
YOUR CELLMATES' HATEFUL LOOKS THAT ARE ALSO SOMEHOW SEDUCTIVE.
THAT REMINDS ME OF SOMETHING A GOOD FRIEND SAID--
AH!
"FUCKING IS BEAUTIFUL. ESPECIALLY IF IT'S WITH A WOMAN."

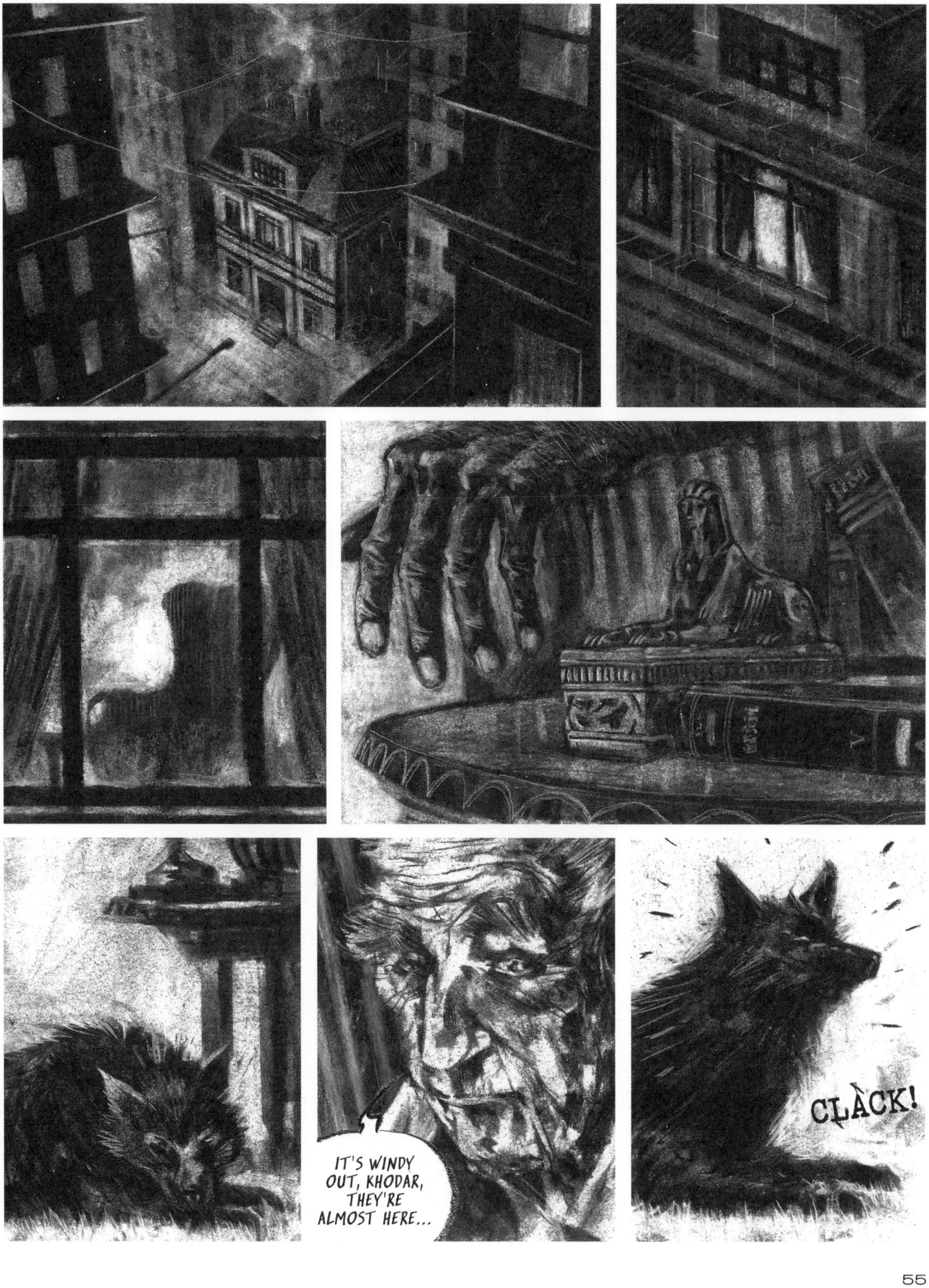
IT'S WINDY OUT, KHODAR, THEY'RE ALMOST HERE...
CLACK!

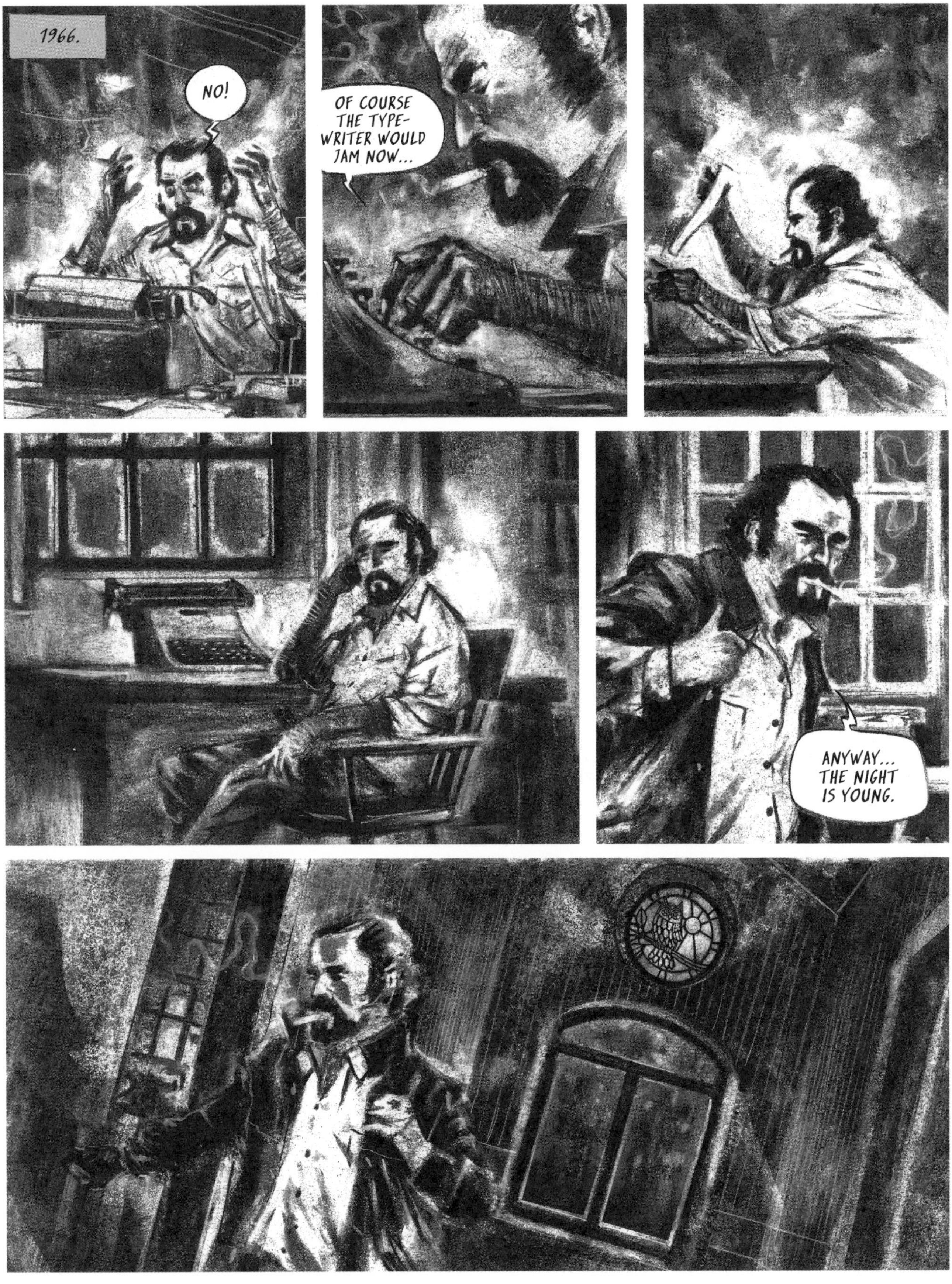
1966.
NO!
OF COURSE THE TYPE-WRITER WOULD JAM NOW...
ANYWAY... THE NIGHT IS YOUNG.

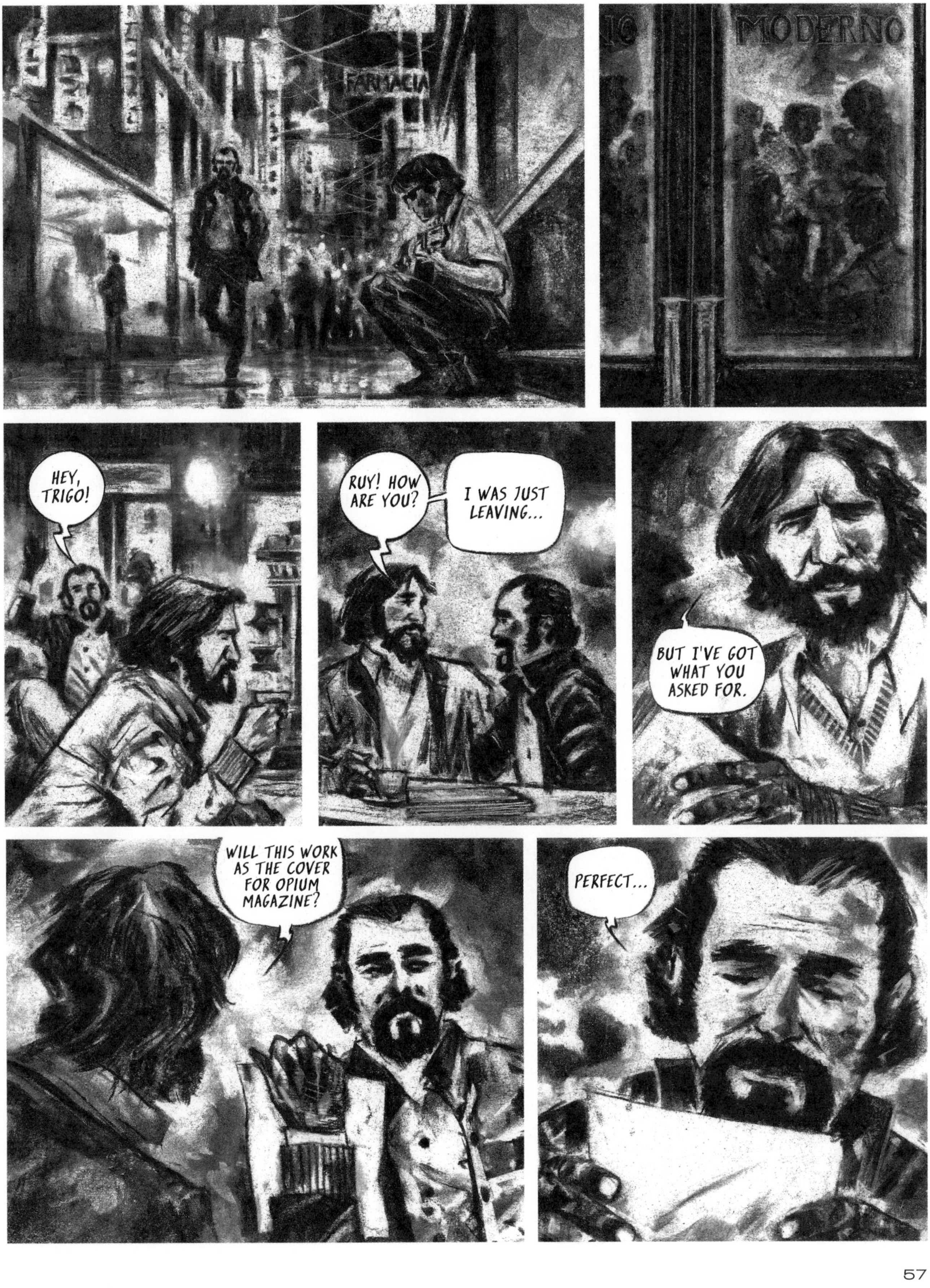

MODERNO
FARMACIA
HEY, TRIGO!
RUY! HOW ARE YOU?
I WAS JUST LEAVING...
BUT I'VE GOT WHAT YOU ASKED FOR.
WILL THIS WORK AS THE COVER FOR OPIUM MAGAZINE?
PERFECT...

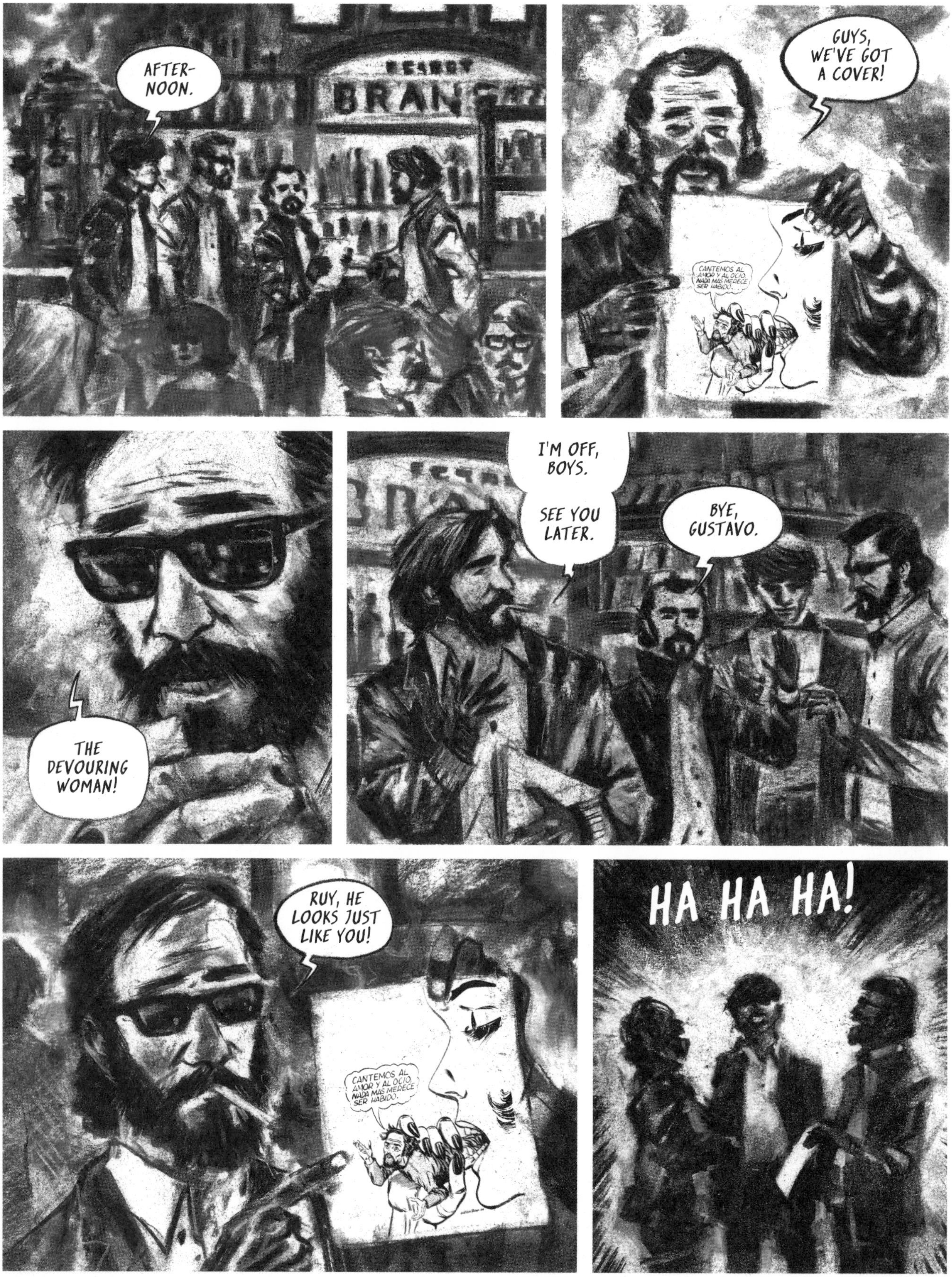
AFTER-NOON.
GUYS, WE'VE GOT A COVER!
CANTEMOS AL AMOR Y AL OCIO, NADA MAS MERECE SER HABIDO.
THE DEVOURING WOMAN!
I'M OFF, BOYS.
SEE YOU LATER.
BYE, GUSTAVO.
RUY, HE LOOKS JUST LIKE YOU!
CANTEMOS AL AMOR Y AL OCIO, NADA MAS MERECE SER HABIDO.
HA HA HA!

IN THE FIRST IMAGE, WE SEE WHAT IS ALMOST CERTAINLY A REPRESENTATION OF DEATH.

IT'S WEARING A HAT SHAPED LIKE A PAGODA ROOF IN A DEPRESSING DARK RED COLOR.

THE OWL LOITERS IN THE STAINED-GLASS WINDOW.

DARK RED PAGODA ROOF AND GREEN FACE. FACE OF A MAN DROWNED IN A RIVER ON A WEEKDAY.

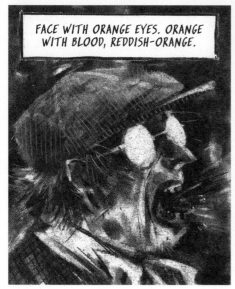

FACE WITH ORANGE EYES. ORANGE WITH BLOOD, REDDISH-ORANGE.

YOU'RE ALWAYS PERCHED ON A BRANCH WATCHING ME.

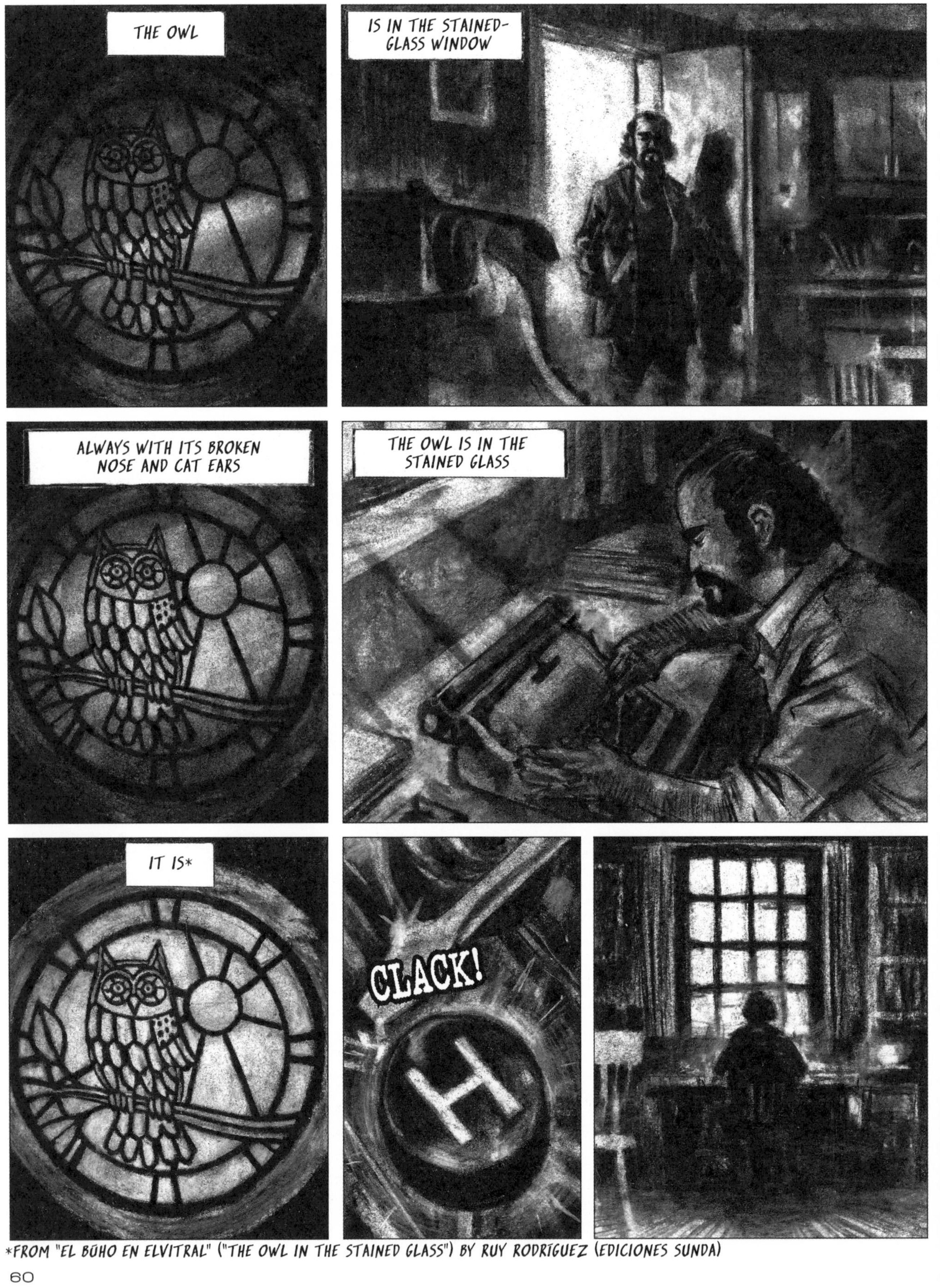
THE OWL
IS IN THE STAINED-GLASS WINDOW
ALWAYS WITH ITS BROKEN NOSE AND CAT EARS
THE OWL IS IN THE STAINED GLASS
IT IS*
CLACK!
H

*FROM "EL BÚHO EN ELVITRAL" ("THE OWL IN THE STAINED GLASS") BY RUY RODRÍGUEZ (EDICIONES SUNDA)

MUSIC SLEEPS TOO.

SOMETIMES FOR CENTURIES.

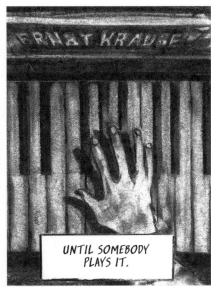

UNTIL SOMEBODY PLAYS IT.

THE NOTES VIBRATE.

THEY COME TO LIFE.

EVERYTHING IS JOY. EXCEPT FOR ANYBODY WHO HATES MUSIC.

NOT AGAIN! GODDAMMIT!

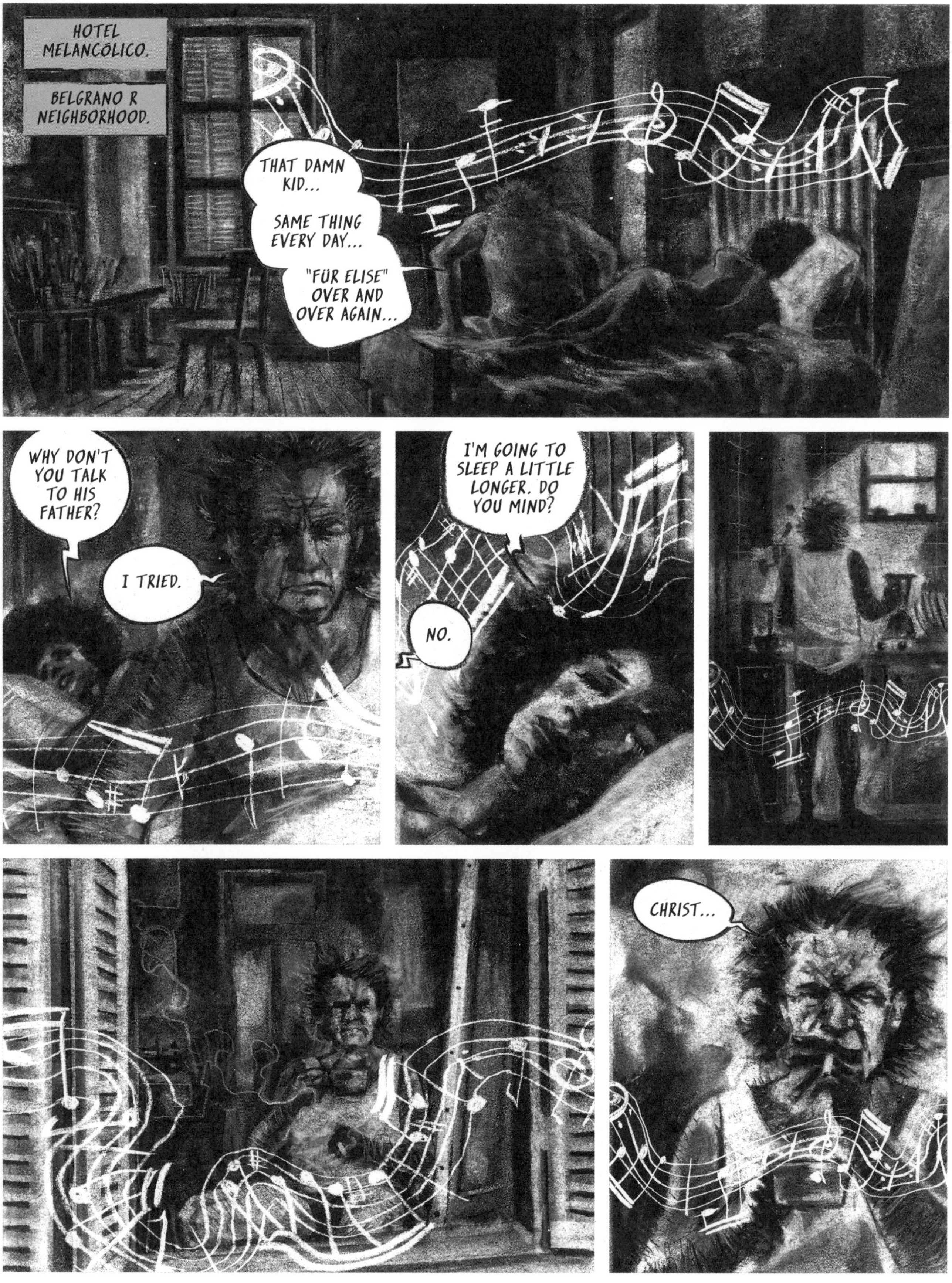
HOTEL MELANCÓLICO.
BELGRANO R NEIGHBORHOOD.
THAT DAMN KID...
SAME THING EVERY DAY...
"FÜR ELISE" OVER AND OVER AGAIN...
WHY DON'T YOU TALK TO HIS FATHER?
I TRIED.
I'M GOING TO SLEEP A LITTLE LONGER. DO YOU MIND?
NO.
CHRIST...

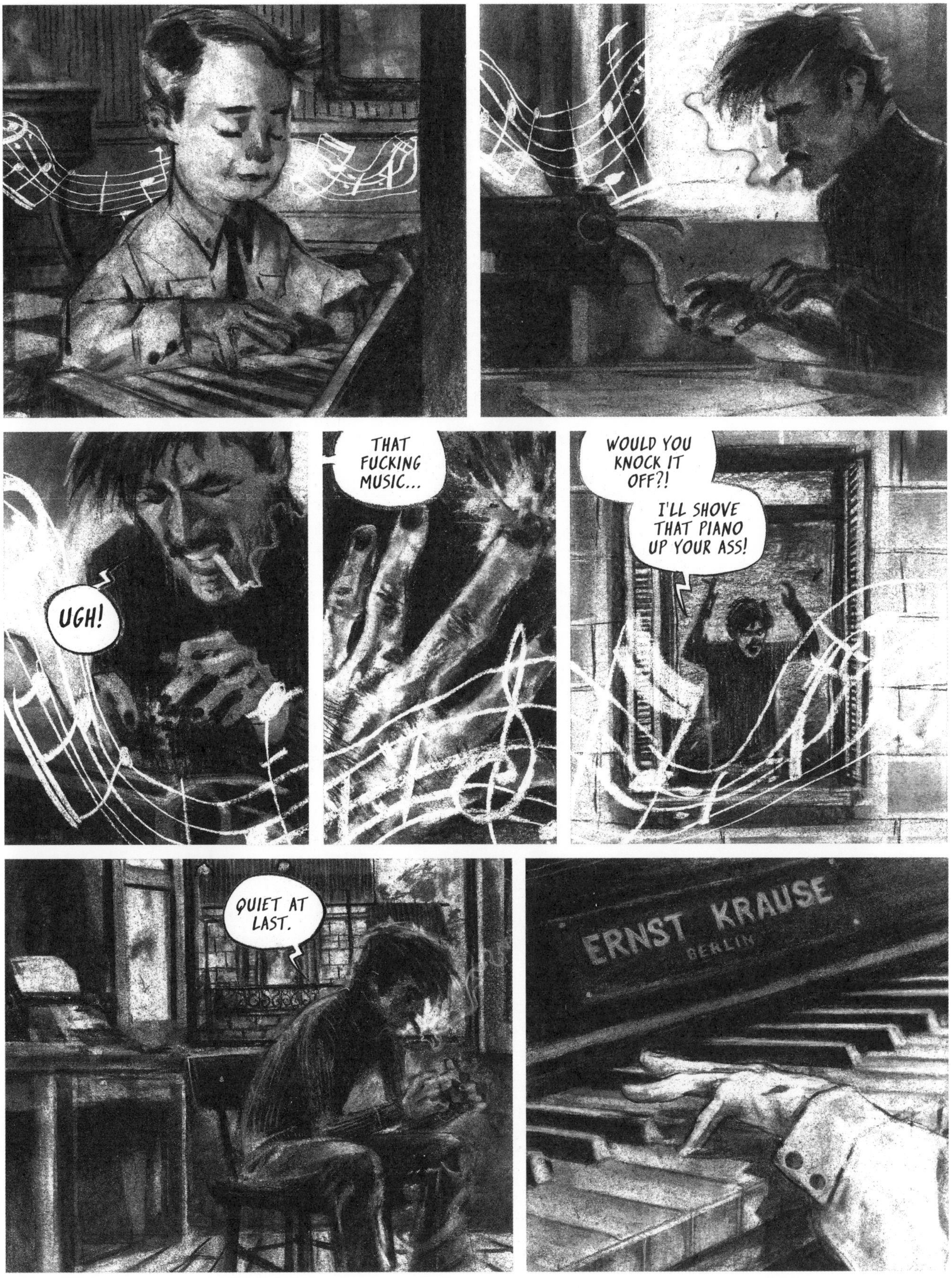
UGH!
THAT FUCKING MUSIC...
WOULD YOU KNOCK IT OFF?!
I'LL SHOVE THAT PIANO UP YOUR ASS!
QUIET AT LAST.
ERNST KRAUSE
BERLIN

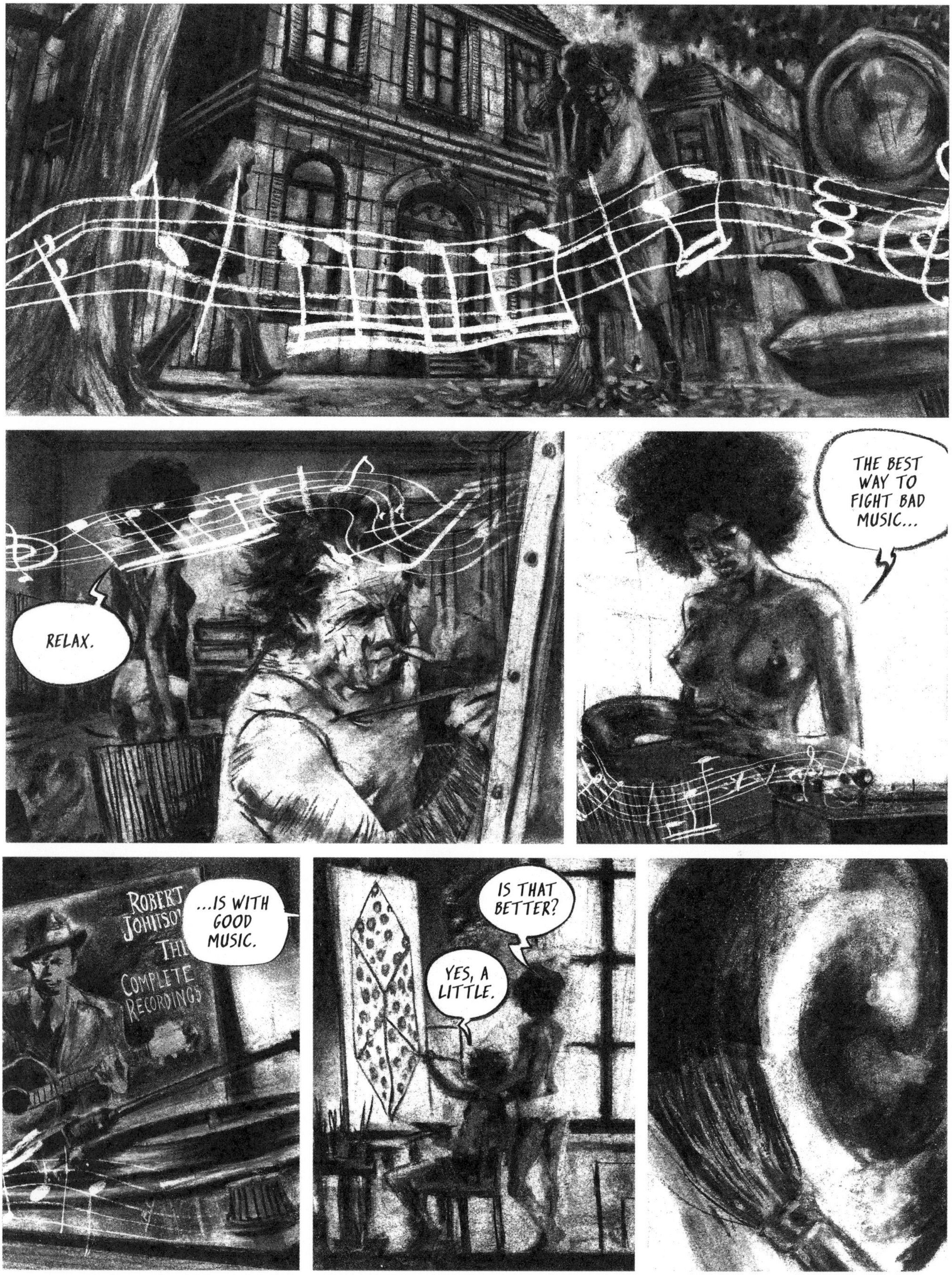
RELAX.
THE BEST WAY TO FIGHT BAD MUSIC...
ROBERT JOHNSON THE COMPLETE RECORDINGS
...IS WITH GOOD MUSIC.
IS THAT BETTER?
YES, A LITTLE.

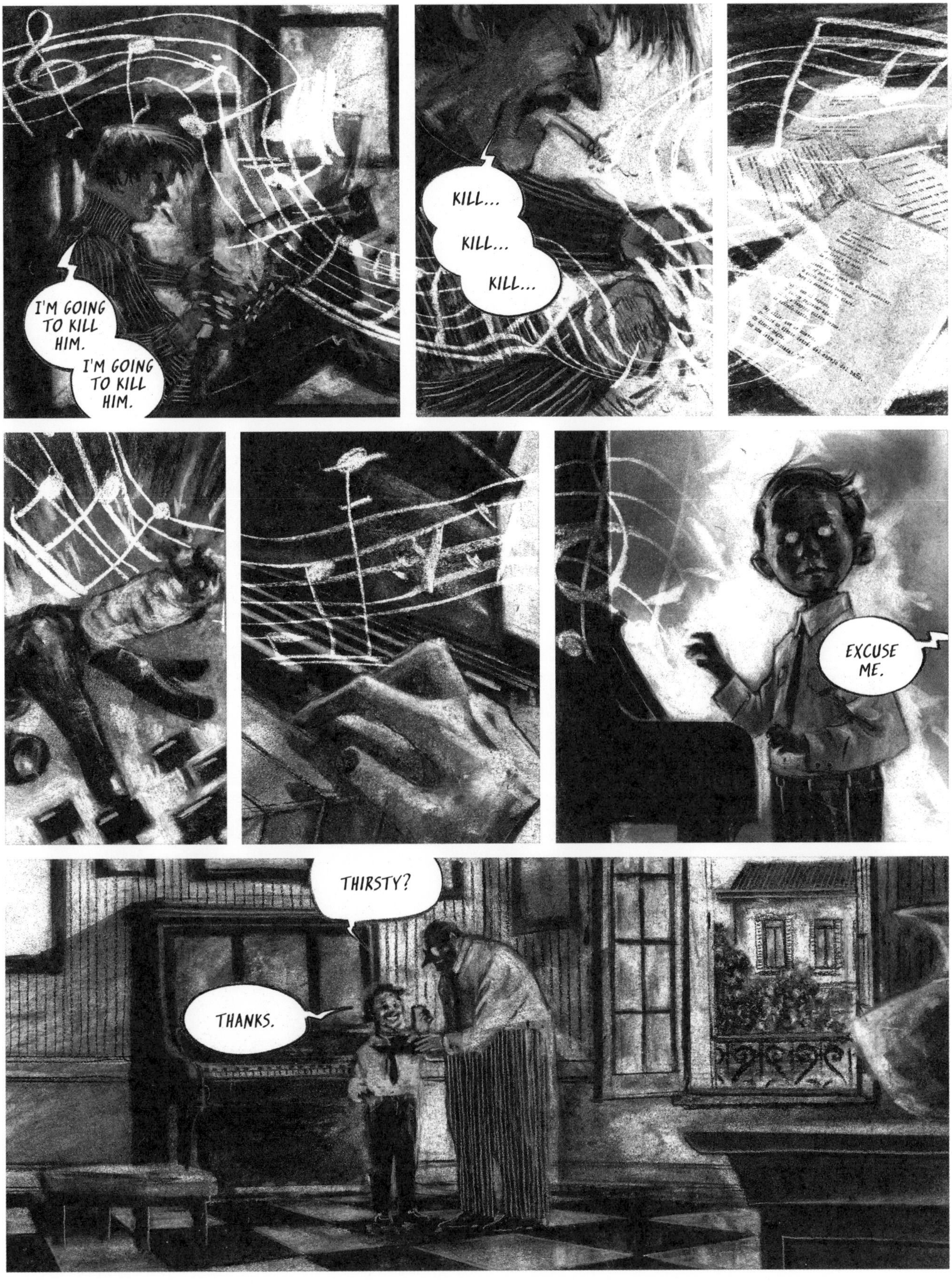
I'M GOING TO KILL HIM.
I'M GOING TO KILL HIM.
KILL...
KILL...
KILL...
EXCUSE ME.
THIRSTY?
THANKS.

AT THE HOTEL MELANCÓLICO THERE WAS A LEGEND.

THE STORY OF A GHOST GIRL WHO USED TO WANDER THE PLACE, MOANING.

BE RIGHT BACK, SWEETIE.

EVERYBODY THOUGHT THAT'S WHAT IT WAS--

A LEGEND.

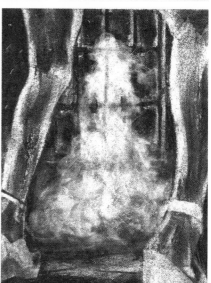

UNTIL THE VEIL OF NIGHT OPENS AND REVEALS ITS ICY MYSTERIES.*

*FROM "POEMAS DEL HOTEL MELANCÓLICO" ("POEMS OF THE HOTEL MELANCÓLOCO") BY MÁXIMO SIMPSON (EDICIONES AMISTAD)

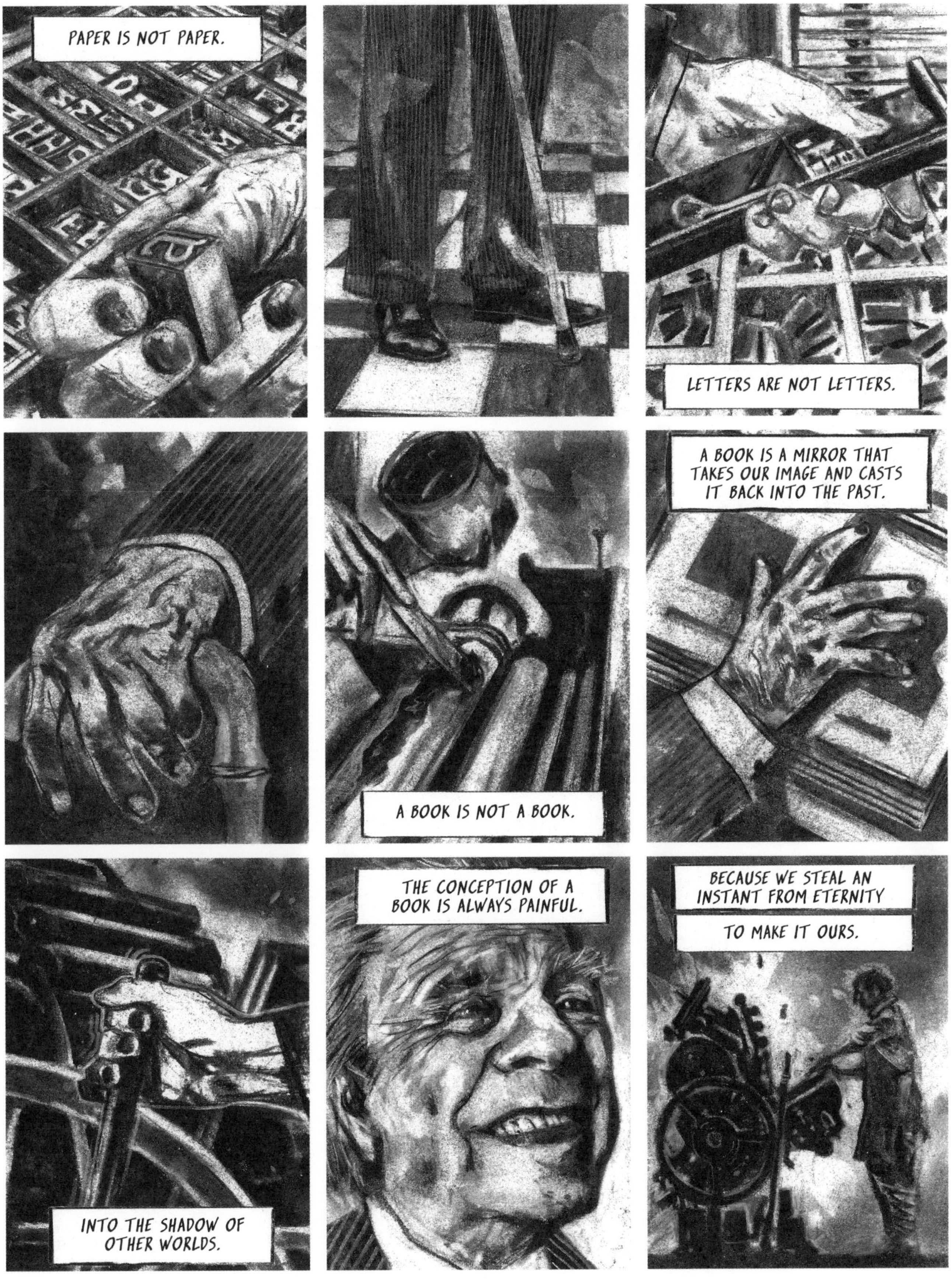
PAPER IS NOT PAPER.
LETTERS ARE NOT LETTERS.
A BOOK IS NOT A BOOK.
A BOOK IS A MIRROR THAT TAKES OUR IMAGE AND CASTS IT BACK INTO THE PAST.
INTO THE SHADOW OF OTHER WORLDS.
THE CONCEPTION OF A BOOK IS ALWAYS PAINFUL.
BECAUSE WE STEAL AN INSTANT FROM ETERNITY
TO MAKE IT OURS.

NATIONAL LIBRARY.

PARIS. 1955.

"FOR THE ALCHEMISTS, SPIRITS ARE REAL INFLUENCES, EVEN IF IN PHYSICAL TERMS THEY ARE ALMOST INTANGIBLE OR IMPONDERABLE."

"THEY ACT IN A MYSTERIOUS MANNER, INEXPLICABLE, UNKNOWABLE, BUT EFFECTIVE...

"...UPON THE SUBSTANCES THAT ARE SUBJECT TO THEIR ACTIONS AND PREPARED TO RECEIVE THEM."

WHAT'S... HAPPENING... TO ME?

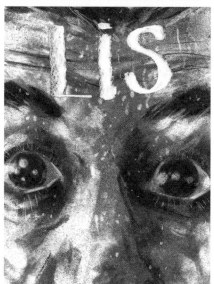

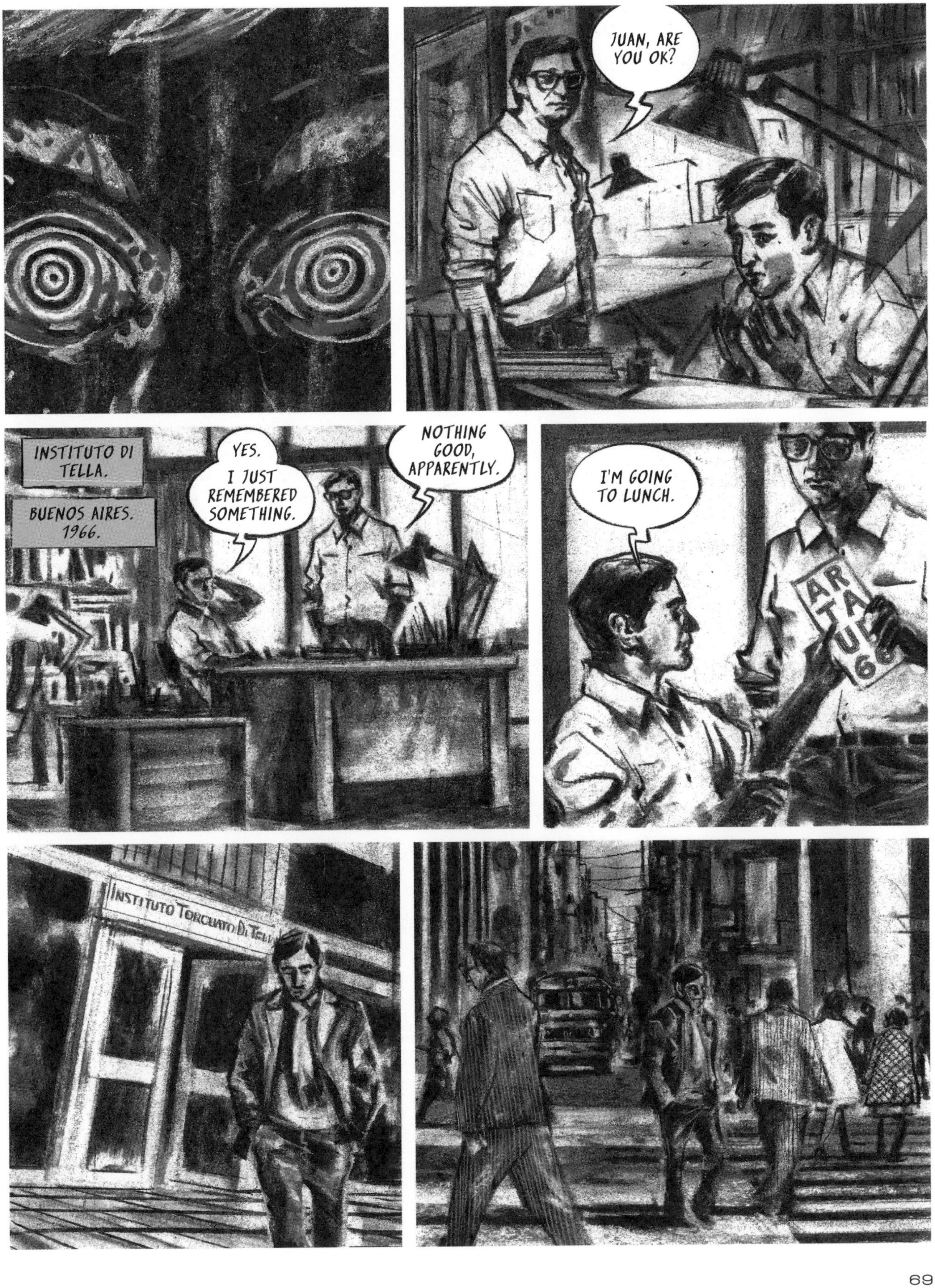

JUAN, ARE YOU OK?
INSTITUTO DI TELLA.
BUENOS AIRES. 1966.
YES. I JUST REMEMBERED SOMETHING.
NOTHING GOOD, APPARENTLY.
I'M GOING TO LUNCH.
ARTAUD 66
INSTITUTO TORCUATO DI TELL

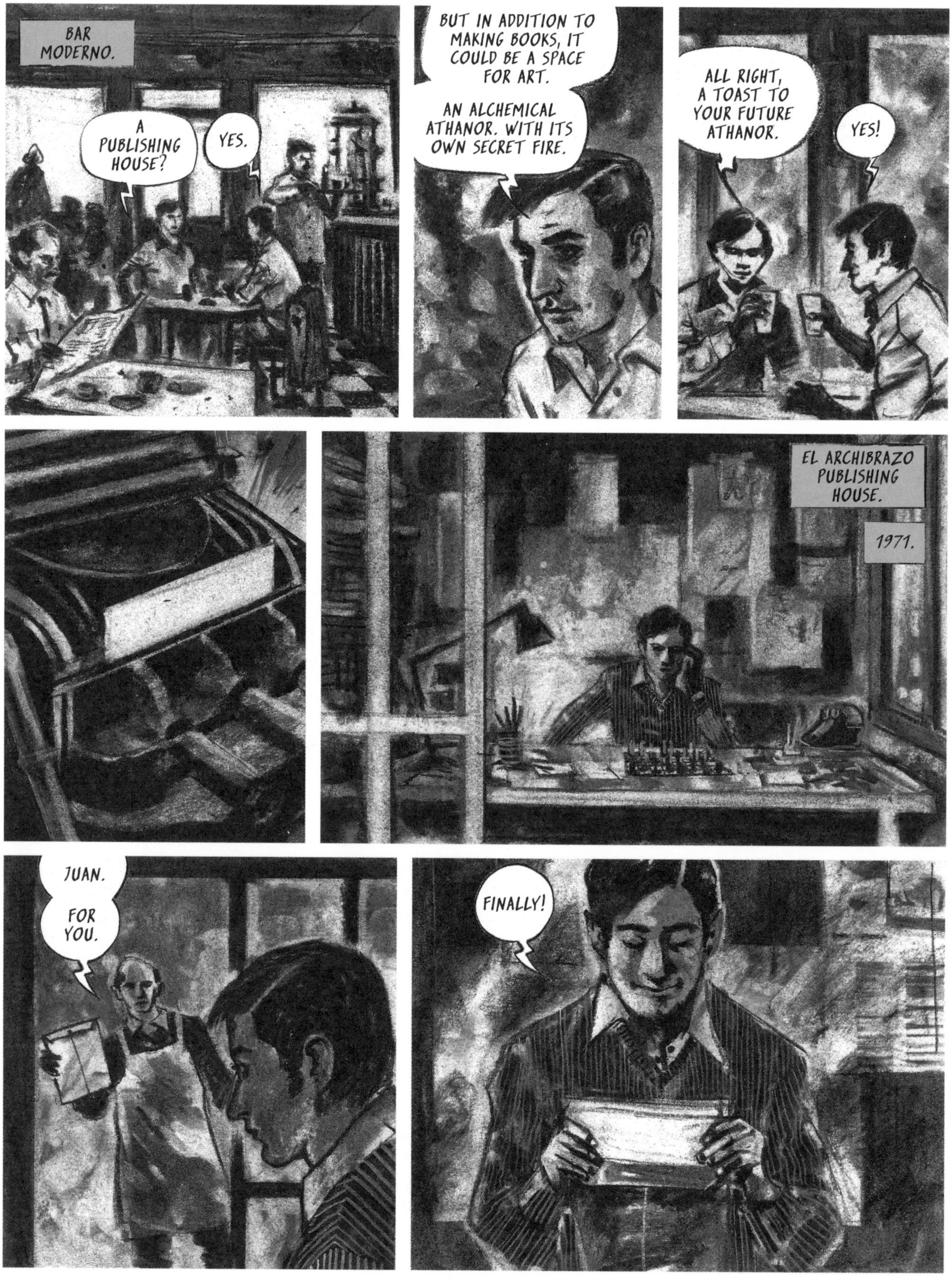
BAR MODERNO.
A PUBLISHING HOUSE?
YES.
BUT IN ADDITION TO MAKING BOOKS, IT COULD BE A SPACE FOR ART.
AN ALCHEMICAL ATHANOR. WITH ITS OWN SECRET FIRE.
ALL RIGHT, A TOAST TO YOUR FUTURE ATHANOR.
YES!
EL ARCHIBRAZO PUBLISHING HOUSE.
1971.
JUAN.
FOR YOU.
FINALLY!

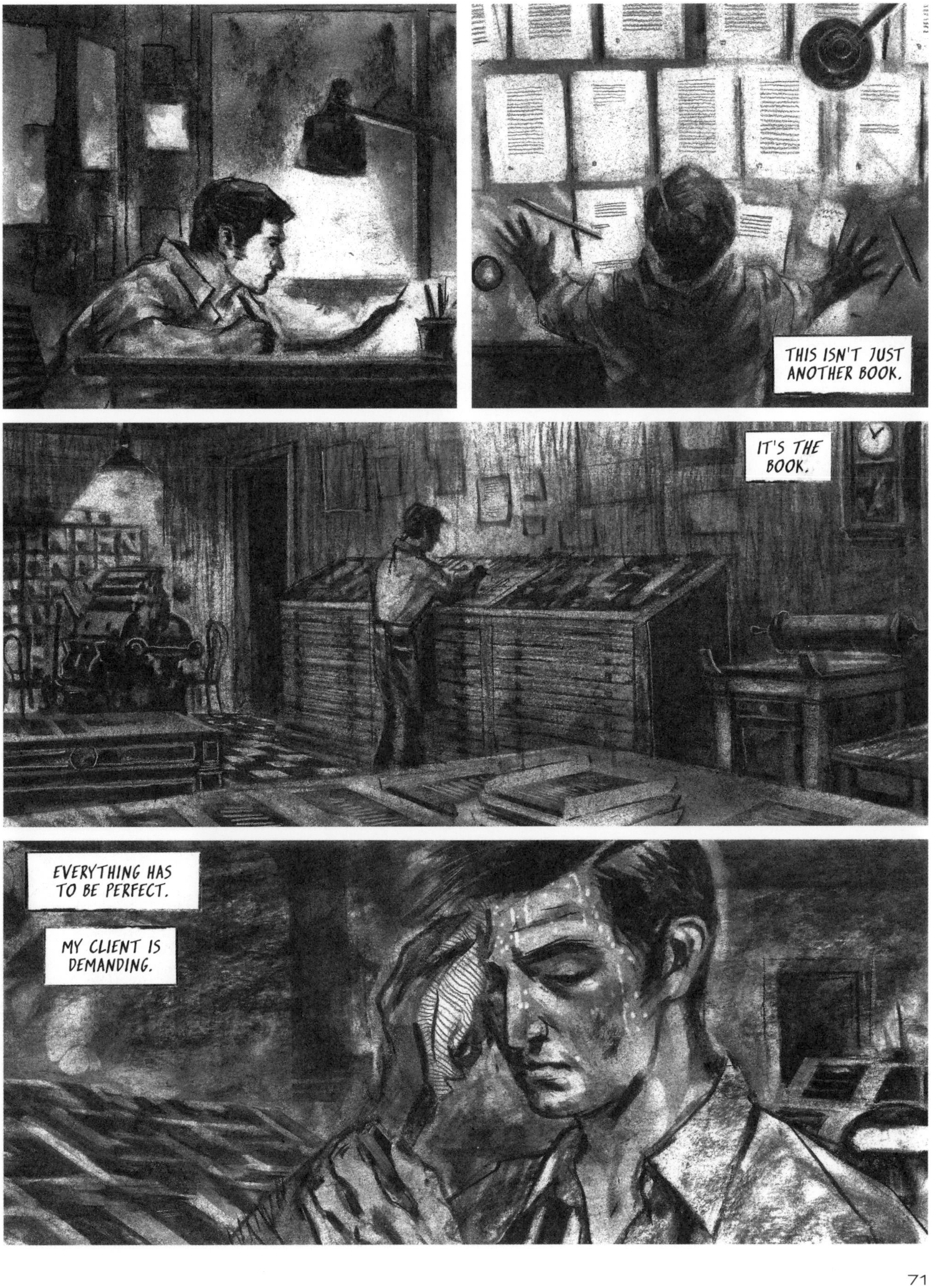
THIS ISN'T JUST ANOTHER BOOK.
IT'S THE BOOK.
EVERYTHING HAS TO BE PERFECT.
MY CLIENT IS DEMANDING.

GOOD AFTERNOON.

AFTERNOON, MR. BORGES. WELCOME TO EL ARCHIBRAZO.

YES.

DO YOU HAVE THE PROOFS FOR MY BOOK?

WE'RE JUST PRINTING THE LAST SIGNATURE.

TO THE TOUCH, AT LEAST, IT SEEMS WONDERFUL...

YOU SEEM A LITTLE UNCOMFORTABLE.

DOES THE NOISE OF THE MACHINES BOTHER YOU?

NO.

QUITE THE OPPOSITE. I'M EXCITED.

AS IF I WERE A SAILOR SUPRISED BY AN INFINITE STORM.

CONGRESO

ARCHIBRAZO EDITOR

BANG!

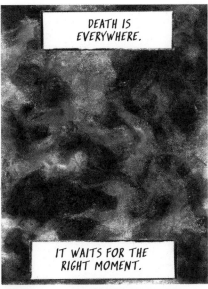

DEATH IS EVERYWHERE.

IT WAITS FOR THE RIGHT MOMENT.

WHICH IS ALWAYS WRONG FOR THE VICTIM.

BUT THAT DOESN'T MATTER.

ART DEMANDS SACRIFICES.

ANONYMOUS BODIES TOSSED TO THE GREAT BEAST

TO SATE ITS ENDLESS APPETITE.

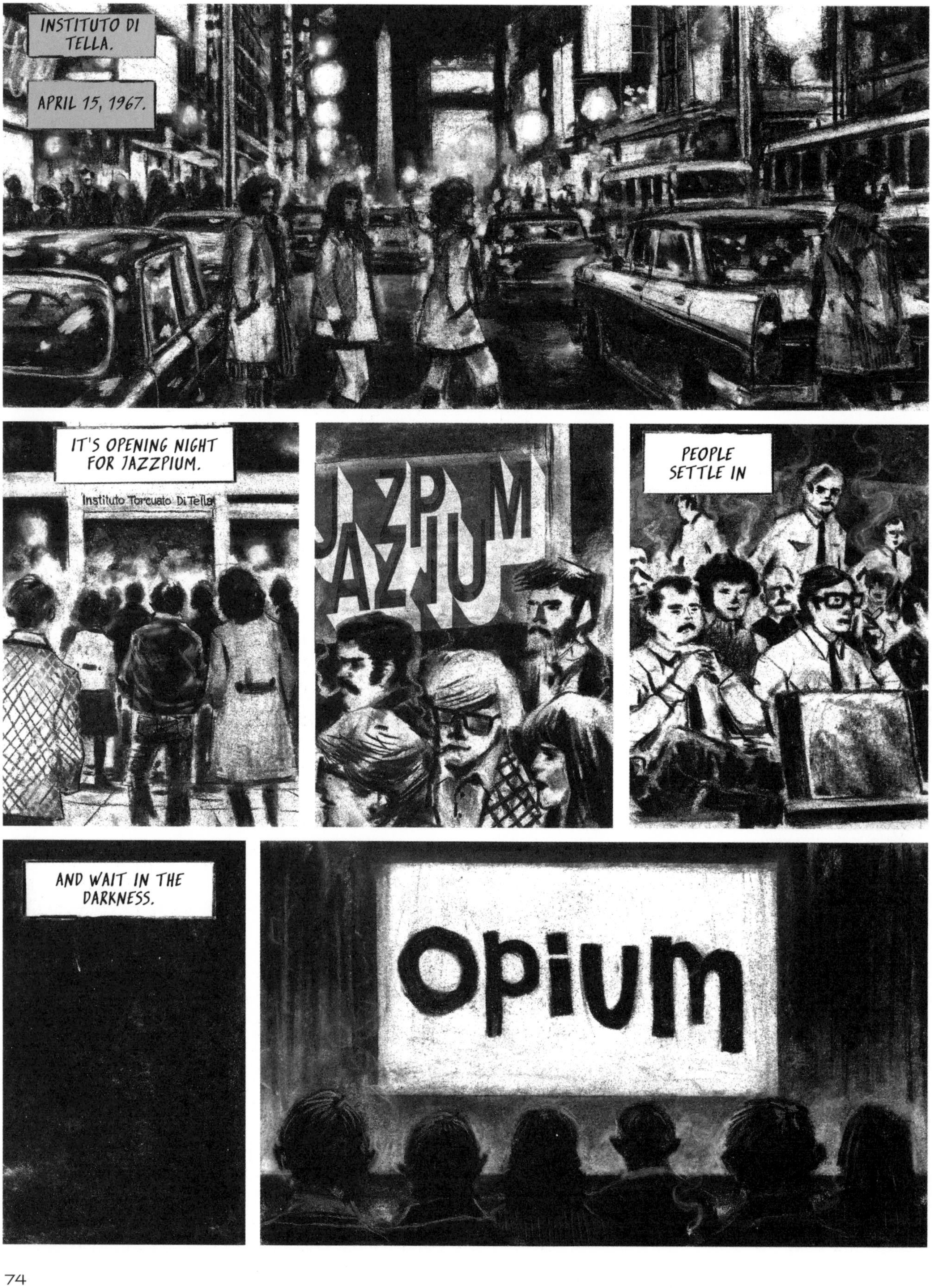
INSTITUTO DI TELLA.
APRIL 15, 1967.
IT'S OPENING NIGHT FOR JAZZPIUM.
Instituto Torcuato Di Tella
PEOPLE SETTLE IN
AND WAIT IN THE DARKNESS.
Opium

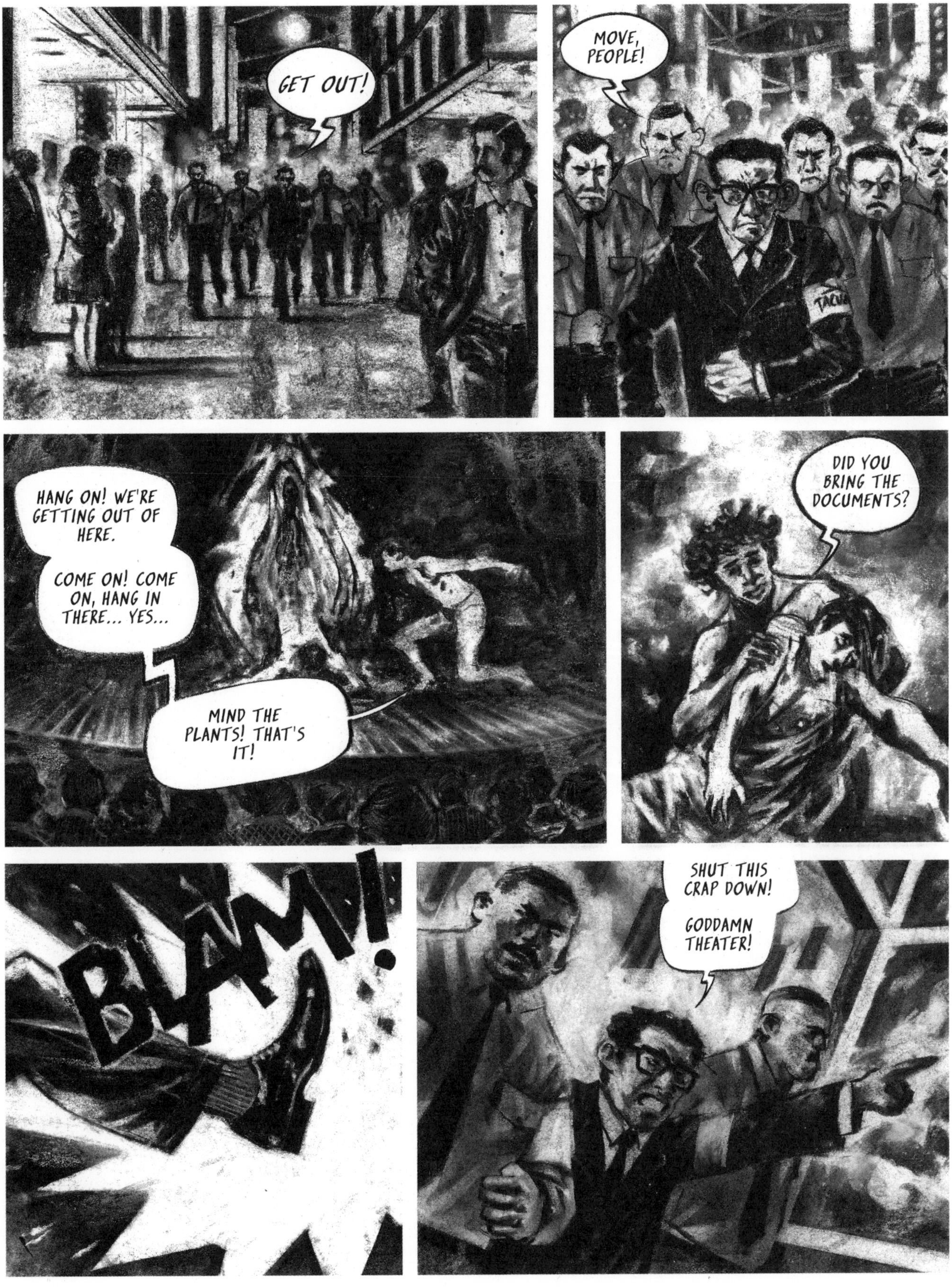
GET OUT!
MOVE, PEOPLE!
HANG ON! WE'RE GETTING OUT OF HERE.
COME ON! COME ON, HANG IN THERE... YES...
MIND THE PLANTS! THAT'S IT!
DID YOU BRING THE DOCUMENTS?
BLAM!
SHUT THIS CRAP DOWN!
GODDAMN THEATER!

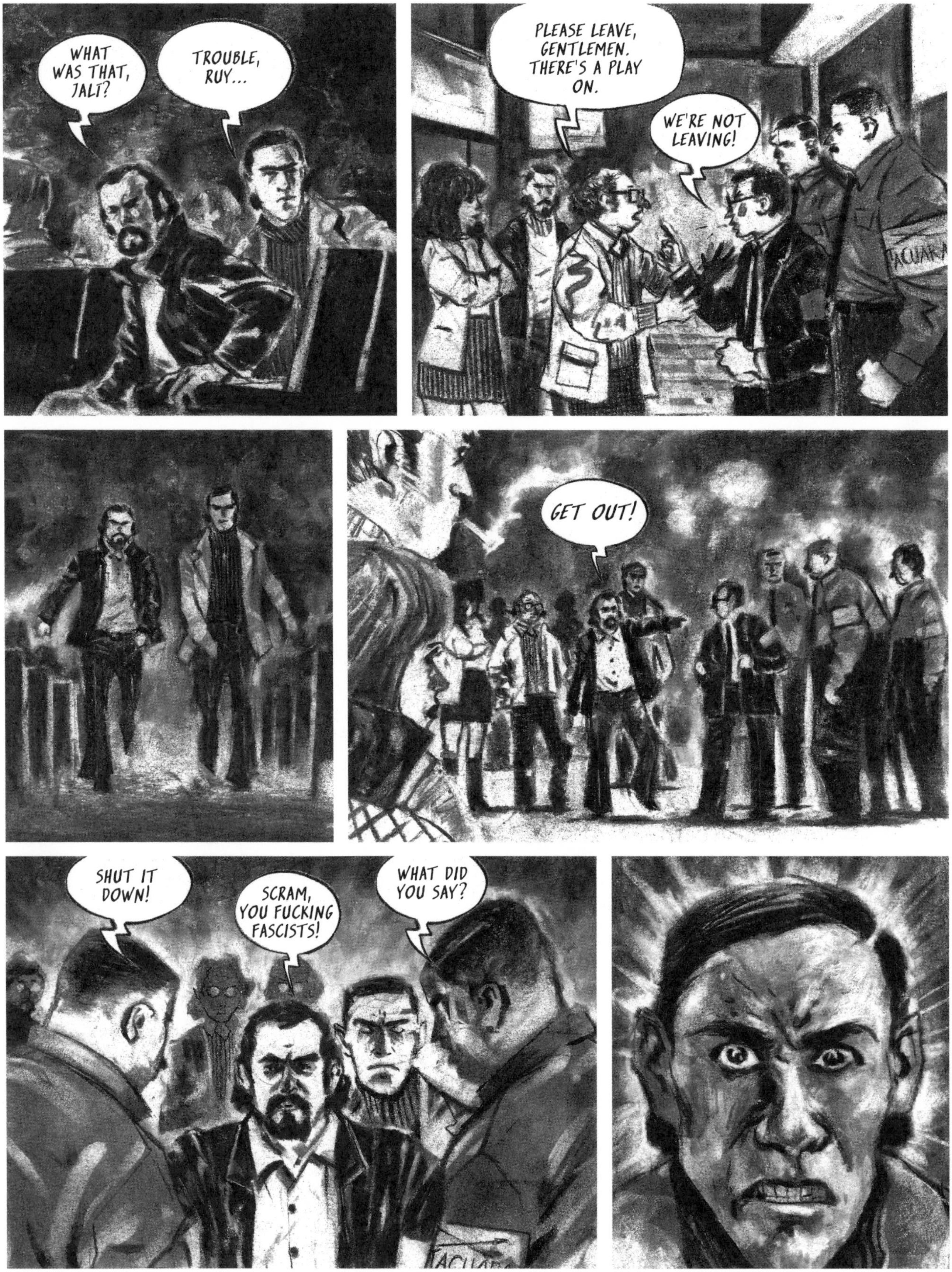
WHAT WAS THAT, JALT?
TROUBLE, RUY...
PLEASE LEAVE, GENTLEMEN. THERE'S A PLAY ON.
WE'RE NOT LEAVING!
GET OUT!
SHUT IT DOWN!
SCRAM, YOU FUCKING FASCISTS!
WHAT DID YOU SAY?

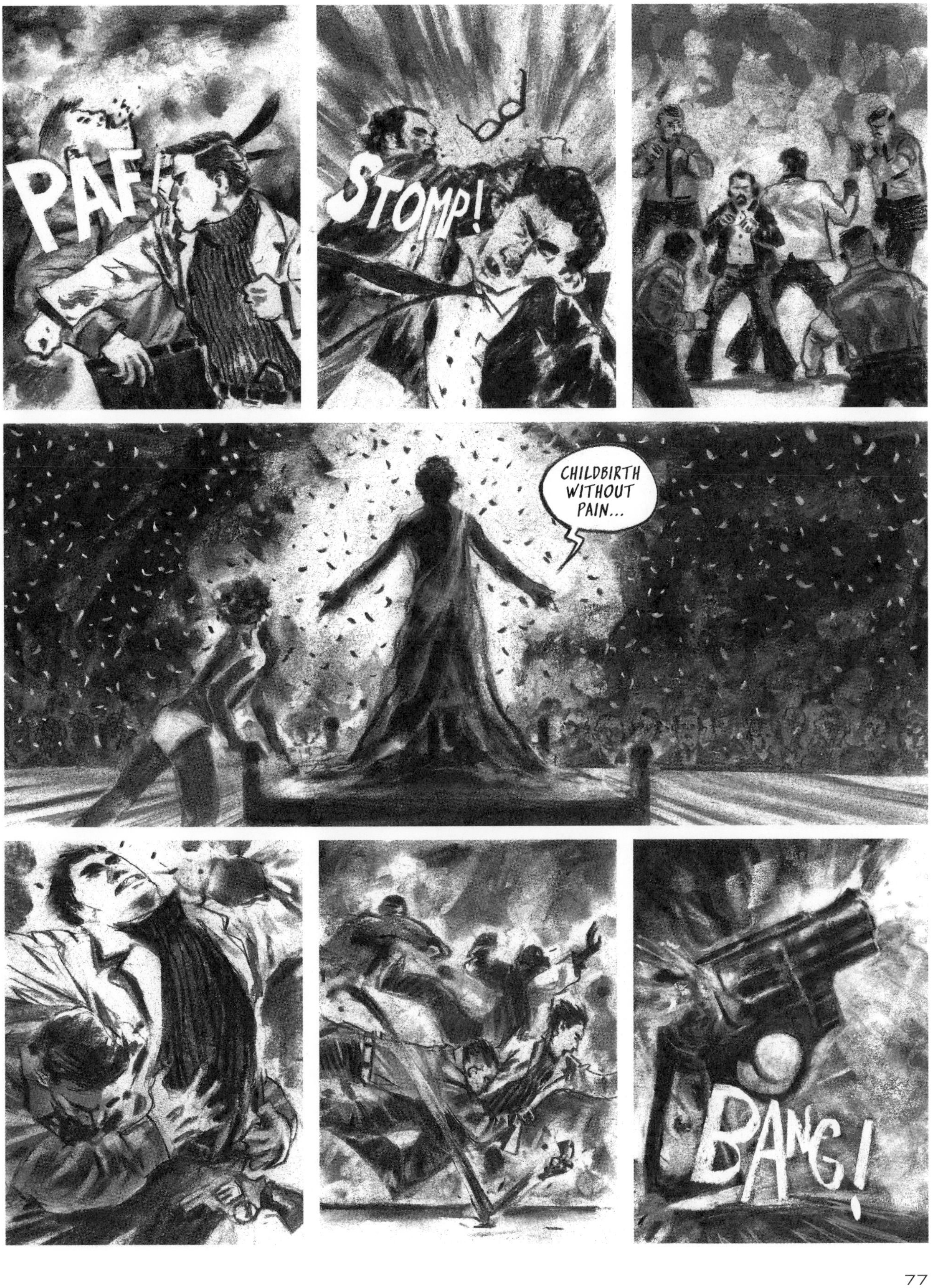
PAF!
STOMP!
CHILDBIRTH WITHOUT PAIN...
BANG!

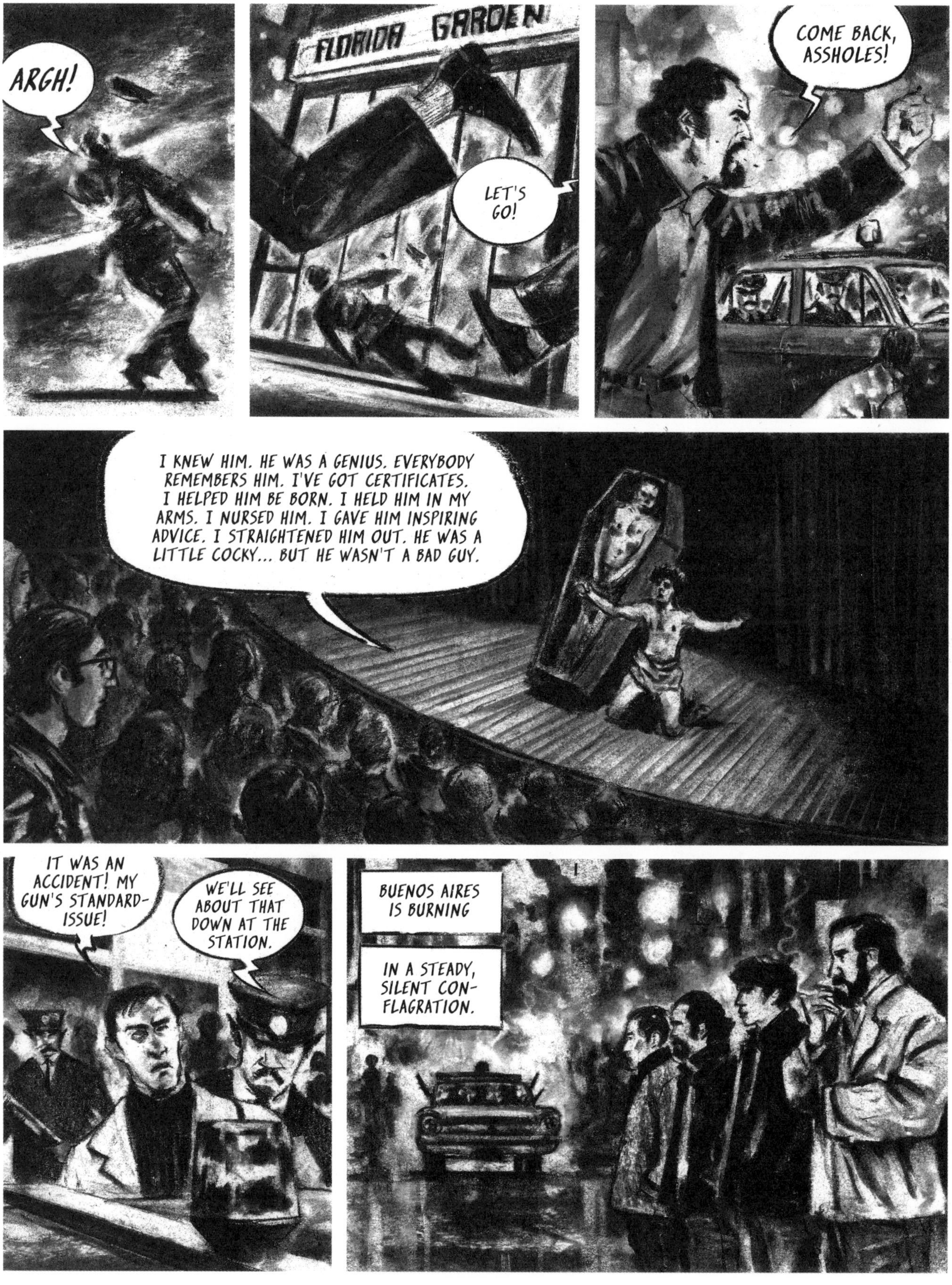
ARGH!
FLORIDA GARDEN
LET'S GO!
COME BACK, ASSHOLES!
I KNEW HIM. HE WAS A GENIUS. EVERYBODY REMEMBERS HIM. I'VE GOT CERTIFICATES. I HELPED HIM BE BORN. I HELD HIM IN MY ARMS. I NURSED HIM. I GAVE HIM INSPIRING ADVICE. I STRAIGHTENED HIM OUT. HE WAS A LITTLE COCKY... BUT HE WASN'T A BAD GUY.
IT WAS AN ACCIDENT! MY GUN'S STANDARD-ISSUE!
WE'LL SEE ABOUT THAT DOWN AT THE STATION.
BUENOS AIRES IS BURNING
IN A STEADY, SILENT CONFLAGRATION.

APP
NDI

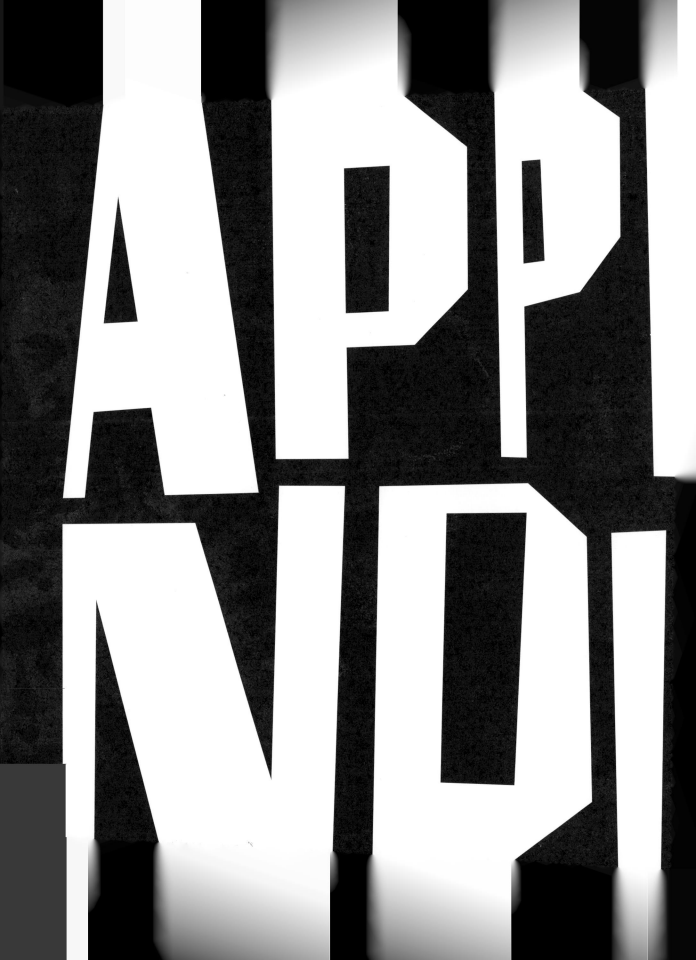

chapter ONE

Buenos Aires, though a relatively young city, was a bastion of esotericism. As early as 1920, the Argentine writer Roberto Arlt had written *Las ciencias ocultas en la ciudad de Buenos Aires* (*The Occult Sciences in the City of Buenos Aires*). Magic had settled in, for good or for ill.

Ithacar Jalí, a volunteer firefighter specializing in explosives by trade, had his own unique worldview. Born on November 6, 1939, with the given name Enrique César Lerena de la Serna, he belonged to the group of artists who swarmed the narrow streets of downtown Buenos Aires in the 1960s. He made paintings in which objects were burning or the firemen were apes, possibly as a sort of catharsis for the intensity of his job.

His fascination with the igneous and the hermetic is apparent in the "Church of the Final Sun," a sort of Buenos Aires cult that he led whose members included writers such as Marcelo Fox and Alberto Laiseca. Jalí was based in the Palermo neighborhood, where he imparted his knowledge and produced a number of booklets and reference books on the occult.

In certain parts of the city, the walls were graffitied with messages like "Jalí is the Final Sun" or covered with wheat-pasted posters that announced: "Everything will be transformed. It is the Time of Radiance and Slaughter. Only the Children of Fire will survive among the flames."

chapter TWO

Marcelo Fox is an enigma.

Everything about him remains swathed in mist, an irresistibly compelling mystery. His only two published books, *Invitación a la masacre* (*Invitation to the Massacre*; 1965) and *Señal de fuego* (*Fire Sign*; 1968), provide insights into an author who told profound stories. To the uninitiated reader, his literature can be deeply unsettling.

Fox was born in Buenos Aires in 1942. His father had a photo processing shop across from what is now Parque Las Heras in the Barrio Norte neighborhood. He was a disciple of Jalí, and his notebooks are full of sketches of swastikas and other mystical symbols. Describing him, the poet Roberto Rapalo wrote that he "never took anything seriously; for him, everything was a joke. It's a shame his early plays, which made us laugh so hard, did not survive, especially *Las monjitas antropófagas o los troskistas siempre traicionan* [*The Cannibal Nuns; or, You Can't Trust a Trotskyite*]. [He] was always trying to freak people out — he wasn't the least bit Nazi. If he'd been French, he'd have been a guru of surrexistentialism, one of his inventions (50% surrealism + 50% existentialism = 100% Foxist madness) — I'm not sure whether its tenets have ever been written down."

The writer Juan-Jacobo Bajarlía said, "In 1967 he came to see me. We hadn't met before. Tall, with a round face, brown eyes, and untidy hair, Marcelo Fox only talked about stomachs. About the lights that come on in the face of insipidness and mediocrity. His prophetic voice, steeped in occultist readings, saw annihilation as the only way to secure the future. The magical order to dissipate old shadows. The moldy murmur of the constellations."

Fox's visceral prose can be seen in stories such as "Adiós, gracias por todo" ("Goodbye, thanks for everything"), where he writes, "I cut my lips shaving. Blood was gushing out. It was sweet. I liked it."

chapter THREE

He always carried his camera with him.

Iaroslav Kosak, or "Iaros," was dubbed "the metaphysical photographer." He was everywhere, taking photos of every detail of Buenos Aires nightlife, from cultural events to informal gatherings.

His archive was extraordinary: more than 300,000 negatives. This photographic treasure trove, according to the writer Juan José Sebreli, was stored in his apartment on Catamarca Street, which was also the setting for the anecdote from "Angel of Death" that led him to be interrogated by the police.

Sebreli's description paints an unmistakable picture of the photographer: "A Ukrainian with a distinctive and hermetic Slavic face, restless eyes, pale blond hair, almost always dressed in black, like a punk before his time. He used to go everywhere, present and at the same time removed from everything that happened, his camera hanging around his neck, ready to record the city's most unusual places."

Over the years, Iaros was evicted numerous times and ended up living out his final days in a tenement in the La Boca neighborhood, and even sometimes on the streets.

His 300,000 negatives, a real prize for urban historians, were left to two of his friends: the photographer Balduzzi and the painter Rómulo Macció, both now deceased.

chapter FOUR

Art forgery: a delicate balance between artistic talent and criminality.

Buenos Aires was no stranger to this shadowy activity; forgeries of Berni and Spilimbergo were sold at a number of galleries both there and in Mar del Plata. In fact, some of those paintings even snuck their way into private collections.

Within that world, "Goldie" (her nickname has been changed for the sake of privacy) moved gracefully yet warily. She produced and sold her copies, eluding the efforts of her victims to catch her along the way.

According to a writer who used to visit her, she had a remarkable beauty that made her much sought after. Though her own work was quite good, she was never able to break out as an artist in her own right.

She was one of the first women in Argentina to wear a miniskirt (which provoked a deluge of insults, catcalls, and other unwanted attentions from men). A friend and lover, a willing comrade in adventure, she discovered the emerging talent of authors such as Alberto Laiseca, whom she first took to the Bar Moderno.

She left her mark on the night alongside other women who forged paths in the art scene.

chapter FIVE

At 76 years old, Hugo Tabachnik published his first book of poetry, *Volviendo a casa (Going Home)*.

Nevertheless, according to the researcher Federico Barea, Hugo was a poet all his life, and was recognized and lived as such.

He was born in Buenos Aires on June 17, 1937. He began studying medicine in 1956, but never became a doctor. He worked as an adman at the prestigious McCann Ericsson agency, but did not pursue that career either. The pull of literature was just too strong. He finally made his debut as a poet in the magazine *El ángel del altillo* (*The Angel in the Attic*). He was one of the many artists who haunted the Bar Moderno and a member of the Sunda group, headed up by the poet Martín "Poni" Micharvegas.

Influenced by American beat poetry, he recounted in an interview, "It was in 1961... surrounded by that dilapidated panel molding — remember? — in Florida, the bar on Viamonte Street, when I heard Leandro Katz read the translation he and Madela Ezcurra had done of Allen Ginsberg's poem "Howl" for the magazine *Airón*, edited by Basilia Papastamatíu. That was my first contact with a poetry that was confessional, raw, breathing, and... it changed my life. ... Of course, it's easy to have something change your life when you're in your twenties..."

He traveled to the United States, where he took a variety of jobs and made contact with the beat poets, including Ginsberg himself. The poet Víctor "Pajarito" Cuello recalls that Tabachnik used to describe the nights of conversation and literary exchange he'd spent with the legendary American writer.

chapter SIX

His greatest work was himself.

Federico Peralta Ramos was born on January 29, 1939, in Mar del Plata, the city founded by his great-grandfather Patricio in 1874.

Raised in an aristocratic family, Ramos soon rebelled against family tradition and sought to forge his own path in art. He created the *Gánica* religion, which proposed that people should always do what they felt like doing, their actions guided solely by their desire. Ramos regularly visited the "Manzana Loca" (Crazy Block), the circle around the Di Tella Institute, a hotbed of Buenos Aires's avant-garde. His deep, somewhat sad eyes were striking.

He was frank in admitting, "I painted without knowing how to paint, wrote without knowing how to write, sang without knowing how to sing. Repeated ineptitude has become my style."

In 1965 he won the Instituto Torcuato Di Tella's National and International Prize, which allowed him to create, in a race against the clock, his most unsettling work: *Nosotros afuera* (*We, the Outsiders*), an enormous egg built of plaster and wood that ended up crumbling in the middle of the exhibition.

During the Sociedad Rural Argentina's 1967 cattle show, he tried to buy a champion bull at auction, without much success. He was awarded a grant by the Guggenheim Foundation, which he promptly squandered with his friends. When the Guggenheim requested an accounting of his expenses, he sent such a frank and categorical letter that from that point on the foundation never again required its grantees to report their expenses.

He loved the poem "La hora de los magos" ("The Hour of the Magicians") by Jorge de la Vega and recited it wherever he could. Ramos also appeared on television, on Buenos Aires's Channel 13, with the legendary humorist Tato Bores.

chapter SEVEN

They had to leave Buenos Aires. And they did.

"They've now left for Central America, those young prophets who, with their charm and smiles, are more destructive than the angel who stood at the gates of Paradise with a laser ray in his hand. May all myths — old and new alike — disappear as they pass through, and in their place may the foliage of Paradise grow

again. Every angel is fearsome from the front, but from behind they're a woman."
(As described in the article "Ritual and Caressing," published in the Colombian
magazine *Nadaismo* in 1971.)

Yoel Novoa and Marta Esviza were footloose actors who threw themselves into
the adventure of traveling Latin America. A road movie, but without a movie. The
road. Obstacles. And theater. Always theater.

To pay for the trip, the writer Abelardo Castillo suggested they organize an art
auction, which was held, after a number of twists and turns, at the Galería del Este.
The auction allowed them to fund their journey, which started in Chile. There, they
spent all their money and debated whether to return to Argentina or keep going.

In the end, mostly hitchhiking, they traveled to Lima, Peru, where they performed
a theater piece that got them arrested. But this event got them a huge amount of
press attention and, once they were released, they sold out their shows. From then
on, they made sure to cause a minor dustup in every country they visited.

Years later, Yoel returned to Buenos Aires, where he worked as a bookseller
and sculptor, holding several exhibitions. As an author, he published the books
Epístola vampírica (*Vampire Epistle*; with illustrations by Alberto Breccia) and *Libro
de vampiros* (*Vampire Book*), among others.

chapter EIGHT

mariani.

Just like that, one name, lowercase.

He was born on January 13, 1936, in Buenos Aires. A nephew of the writer Roberto
Mariani, he was steeped in literature from the start. In addition to the books his
uncle gave him, his home was filled with many adventure novels and socialist and
anarchist political pamphlets.

He later confessed that the biggest influences on his poetry were Franz Kafka and
Ezra Pound. From the latter, he took the spiritual motto of the magazine *Opium*:
"Sing we for love and idleness, naught else is worth the having."

mariani's style was whimsical, intense, carnal, and his poems were a game. The
reader had to descend into the words and play with them, to find, perhaps, the
true meaning.

"*así*	(thus
desnudo i despojado de membrete,	naked and stripped of a letterhead,
se apresta a regresar al origen de su noche.	he hastens back to the origin of his night.
regresar	once more
a beber.	to drink.
a beber entre los muslos de su amante, de noche,	to drink between his lover's thighs, at night,
la historia de su vida en l acecho diluida."	the story of his life dissolved in waiting.)

He participated as an actor in the legendary movie *Tiro de gracia* (*Coup de Grâce*;
Ricardo Becher, 1969). His books include *Siete historias bochornosas* (*Seven Shameful
Stories*) and *Siete poemas grassificantes* (*Seven Grassifying Poems*), among others. He
lived in Brazil, splitting his time among São Paulo, Rio de Janeiro, and Búzios. He
later resided in Spain and then returned to Argentina, where he lived in Zapala,
Neuquén Province, until his death in August 2004.

chapter NINE

"tenemos una amiga en la ciudad
esa amiga es la violencia
la misma del puño de mi hermano de
*   siete años matando a dios*
con tenazas de herrero"

(we have a friend in the city
that friend is violence
the same violence that's in my seven-
   year-old brother's fist as he slays god
with blacksmith pincers)

Sergio Mulet's poetry was swift and furious. Almost like a slap in the reader's face, leaving them dazed and disconcerted. This fragment comes from "Poema I" ("Poem I"), published in the second issue of *Opium* magazine in 1965.

Mulet was born in Marsella, Spain, in 1942. He was the son of Spanish refugees who traveled to Buenos Aires in search of a new life. He, Ruy Rodríguez, and Reynaldo Mariani formed the Opium group, dubbing themselves "writers who don't write."

The author of *Soy tu patrón* (*I'm Your Boss*; 1966) and *Tiro de gracia* (*Coup de Grâce*; 1969), Mulet also worked as a stage and screen actor, which allowed Opium to increase its reach.

Because of his good looks, his friend Yoel Novoa recalls, "As young men, going around the Moderno and the Di Tella, we studied each other's appearance. Later we'd run into each other at parties, at openings and inaugurations, and I was always by Sergio's side, supporting Sergio. He would have been a couple of years older than me, but in terms of his height and looks, he was way ahead. He wasn't much of a talker; he remained inscrutable, and at the end of any interaction, he might smile or let loose a profanity, but it was rare for him to say anything longer than that."

He enjoyed boxing, he worked as a journalist, and his life was as intense as his writing. He was thrown in jail in Bolivia, and requested and was granted asylum in Spain. There, according to some accounts, he eventually started working as a bodyguard. But he never stopped writing. He visited Martín "Poni" Micharvegas, who has fond memories of him.

Violence followed him even to the end: he was murdered in Romania in 2007.

chapter TEN

"Tienes ojos tristes, ojos que se expanden
en fuga, ojos que hacen fiestas de todos los
elogios. no ejerzas profesión de triste, baila
aunque no suene mi trompeta, mírame y
baila en tu espacio ortopédico."

(You've got sad eyes, eyes that expand
in flight, eyes that turn all praise into
celebrations. You're not sad by profes-
sion—dance even though my trumpet
isn't sounding, look at me and dance
in your orthopedic space.)

These words come from *El búho en el vitral* (*The Owl in the Stained Glass Window*; Sunda, 1967), the only book published by Ruy Rodríguez, cofounder of the Opium group.

Born on April 22, 1940, Ruy was a denizen of the Buenos Aires nightlife, frequenting smoky bars where people lived poetry.

Besides his work with *Opium* magazine, he also wrote comic book scripts. He was a friend of Gustavo Trigo, the legendary cartoonist who worked at the Columba and Récord publishing houses, among others, and ended up settling in Italy.

Under the pseudonym Ovid Allat, Ruy developed the first script for the series *Arcano XIII*, which was set in New York and Paris and dealt with occult themes. The project was offered to Récord, but the negotiations with the editor fell through.

The first page of this chapter is from that comic book script, which was never drawn.

chapter ELEVEN

It was not a hotel. It was a stronghold where painters, filmmakers, poets — all manner of artists living on the fringe of Argentine society — took refuge. A place to take a break from bustling, often unstable daily life.

Its official name was the Hotel Suiza, but everybody called it the Hotel Melancólico. It was located on 3039 Sucre Street, in the affluent Belgrano R neighborhood of Buenos Aires. Described as a dilapidated mansion, its affordable rooms lodged common folk as well as artists who later became famous, such as the Chilean songwriter Violeta Parra.

The owner of the hotel was known as Madame Vadim and, according to the poet Máximo Simpson, who lived there for three years, she was an elderly woman, the daughter of a Russian general who had served the tsar.

Nights at the Hotel Melancólico were electric: musical performances and lectures, raucous affairs and more subdued gatherings that involved listening to the radio or reading in silence. Anything could happen there... and did. Even, as described by Opium's Ruy Rodríguez, the mysterious appearance of the ghost of a young woman whose identity was never established.

chapter TWELVE

A font is much more than a style, a way of presenting symbols that, when put together, form words.

A font is a ceremony; anyone who performs it can engage in a unique dialogue with the future reader. A communion between strangers.

Juan Ioannis Andralis was, among other professions, a publisher. His El Archibrazo venture, which is still in operation (now as a sociocultural center), located at 441 Mario Bravo Street, housed a printing press that produced books that are today considered sacred relics. These include the first edition of *El Congreso* (*The Congress*) by Jorge Luis Borges.

Andralis had been part of the French surrealist movement, had traveled into the heart of mysticism and magic and returned from Europe to Buenos Aires, where he worked side by side with Mario Pellegrini, son of the great poet and art critic Aldo Pellegrini. Together they founded the Editorial Argonauta publishing house.

As part of the Instituto Di Tella's Graphics Department, Andralis designed a large number of pamphlets related to exhibitions and the works presented in them. Even in the 21st century, these visual artifacts continue to strike us with their simplicity and power.

Though he departed physically in 1994, Andralis is still alive among us, not just in our memories but in his own font: Andralis ND.

chapter THIRTEEN

Fire doesn't just consume. It also scars. It leaves its igneous mark on things.

Although Opium, the group of writers who didn't write, who hurled their cries into the night, mainly published magazines for distribution and exchange with others, they eventually ventured into theater as well.

Unfamiliar with the mechanisms of playwriting and theatrical production, they developed *Jazzpium* (the full script can be read in the General Society of Authors of Argentina's library in Buenos Aires). *Jazzpium* could be described as a work of experimental theater, or audio-visual-performative — and especially musical — experimentation. Directing the work fell to Norman Briski.

The production opened on Saturday, April 15, 1967. It was a chaotic night. According to Ruy Rodríguez, a group of nationalists showed up at the Instituto Di Tella and tried to shut the play down. There was a scuffle, and Jalí brandished his official-issue firearm (he was a firefighter) to scare off the intruders. In the confusion, Jalí fell and his gun went off, killing the 21-year-old police officer Dionisio Américo Navarro, who was standing guard nearby.

The accident was described as follows: "The report is expected to show whether the bullet that struck him came from the weapon of a spectator at the Di Tella performance, Enrique César Llerena (Argentine, 25 years old, an officer with the Buenos Aires provincial police and a volunteer firefighter in Vicente López), who started firing indiscriminately when he found himself surrounded by a group of Tacuaristas [members of Tacuara, an Argentine far-right guerrilla movement] ... He was there to see the show *Jazzpium*, by Norman Briski. The men who burst into the building hurled insults at the 30 people waiting for the program to start and praised Tacuara and Hitler."

Later, once the matter had been cleared up, Jalí continued his artistic endeavors and ended up becoming a veterinarian specializing in dogs. He was also a huge heavy metal fan.

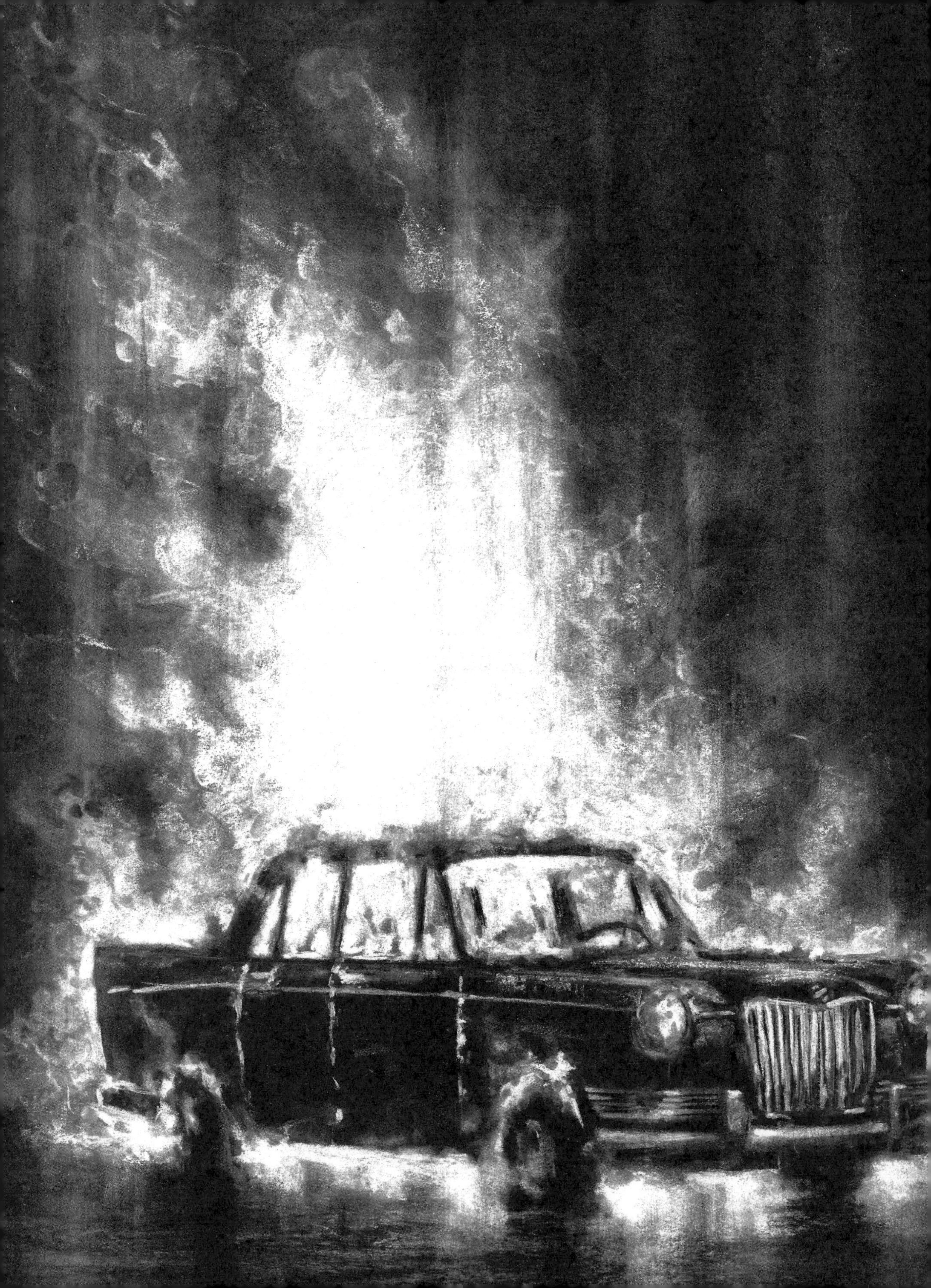